SAINT FRANCIS

OF PAOLA

God's Miracle Worker Supreme

Mrs. Roberta Davis
240 Exeter Rd
PO Box 48
Lebanon, CT 06249

SAINT FRANCIS OF PAOLA

God's Miracle Worker Supreme
(1416-1507)

by

Gino J. Simi

and

Mario M. Segreti

*Heal the sick, raise the dead, cleanse the lepers,
cast out devils: freely have you received, freely
give. Do not possess gold, nor silver, nor money
in your purses.*

Matthew 10:8-9

TAN BOOKS AND PUBLISHERS, INC.
Rockford, Illinois 61105

NIHIL OBSTAT:

Rev. Msgr. Henry J. Yannone
Censor Deputatus

IMPRIMATUR:

William Cardinal Baum
Archbishop of Washington
Washington, D.C.,
December 27, 1976

The *nihil obstat* and *imprimatur* are official declarations that a book or pamphlet is free of doctrinal or
moral error. No implication is contained therein that
those who have granted the *nihil obstat* and the *imprimatur* agree with the content, opinions or statements
expressed.

Library of Congress Catalog Card Number: 77-78097

ISBN: 0-89555-065-2

Anyone who has received signal favors from or has
been the recipient of miracles through the intercession
of St. Francis of Paola should write the details and send
them to Santuario di Paola, Paola (Cosenza) Calabrio,
Italy 87027.

The picture on the cover was painted by G. B. Piazzetta (1682-1754) and hangs in the Pinacoteca di
Padova, Italy.

Printed and bound in the United States of America.

TAN BOOKS AND PUBLISHERS, INC.
P.O. Box 424
Rockford, Illinois 61105

1977

About the Authors

Gino J. Simi and Mario M. Segreti are both natives of Italy. Mr. Simi was born in Lucca in 1902 and immigrated to the United States in 1909 with his parents, his sister, and his two brothers. He went to high school here and later attended American and George Washington Universities. He spent ten years on the editorial staff of the old *Washington Times* and later worked for several agencies of the Federal Government as an information officer. He then became Director and Executive Secretary of the D.C. Apprenticeship Council. He has three children, a son and two daughters, all of whom are married. He is presently retired and living with his wife in the Washington suburb of Bethesda, Maryland, where he engages in free-lance writing and editing for several periodicals.

Mr. Segreti was born in Belmonte Calabro, Cosenza in Southern Italy, the youngest of eight children. At the age of fifteen, upon graduating from high school, he came to the United States with his family and settled in Washington, where his father had preceded the family. During World War II, he served in the Army—two years in the Persian Gulf Command and one year in the China-Burma-India Theater. After the War he joined his brothers in the family business, Segreti Brothers Stone Contractors, as a junior partner, later becoming a senior partner and estimator. He presently owns a food service business and lives in Bethesda, Maryland with his wife and their two children.

Messrs. Simi and Segreti have enough background material on the life of Saint Francis of Paola to write a definitive biography and have promised to do one if this popularly oriented biography is sufficiently well received.

Table of Contents

Foreword

Saint Francis was born in Paola, Calabria, Italy, fifteen miles or so from my own birthplace, Belmonte Calabro. It may be due to the proximity of the two towns that the veneration in which he was held by all the Calabrians manifested itself so ardently in the hearts of the good people among whom I spent my early years. I remember first being told of him by my dear mother when I was only five or six years old. As I grew, I learned from her and from my elders in our parish more and more about Saint Francis of Paola and about the many miracles he had wrought with the help of God.

After my immigration to America, I became more and more aware with the passing years how precious little is generally known here concerning this saint and miracle worker. A few years ago I went back to Italy to visit my sister Rose and others of my relatives and to renew friendships with some of my school companions. Yet it was not until a few months later, after my return to America, that, having come upon a medal of Saint Francis of Paola, I paused to do some thinking. I have been close to the Church all my life and have read the lives of many saintly people, but none has inspired in me a deeper reverence than has the life of this great saint—largely because of the compassion and love he bore for his fellow man and because of the many miracles which he worked.

I had long known about a number of books and publications in Latin, Italian, French and Spanish concerning Saint Francis, but when I tried to find works written in English—either original texts or translations—I found nothing. Three years ago, I asked Gino J. Simi, a retired newspaper writer who had worked for the old *Washington Times* and also a very dear friend of many years, whether

9

he would be interested in collaborating with me in writing
a book in English about this man of God. Not to my surprise, Mr. Simi indicated he did not know much about
Saint Francis of Paola. However, after I recounted what I
had learned concerning him, he showed great interest in
what I was seeking to do and promised to help me. It is
through his expertise as a writer and because of the time he
was able to devote to it that this book has been made possible.

Our task of obtaining the needed material about Saint
Francis was greatly aided by and therefore we are deeply
indebted to Professor Emilio Frangella of Longobardi, a
high school companion of mine and editor of *Calabria Let-
teraria*. He gathered together and sent me a large number
of books and publications in Latin and Italian.

Saint Francis patterned and shaped his life after that of
his favorite saint, Saint Francis of Assisi. Moreover, he
gave the order he founded the name "Minimi," the
"Least," that is, more humble than the "Minori" founded
by the great Saint of Assisi. He worked his miracles, not to
create a sensation, nor for personal glory or reward, but to
fulfill the urge of a boundless love and compassion for all
mankind. He was of peasant stock and would have preferred above all else to spend his days in prayer and in penance, to be known and remembered only as a humble friar.
However, because of the suffering and abuses to which his
people were subjected during the fifteenth century, he
came out of the forest, which had been his home and his
chapel, and brought love of God, Christian joy, and most
of all, charity, to his fellow men.

That Saint Francis of Paola is not generally known to
the English-speaking world is to a large degree the fault of
all of us who immigrated here from Calabria. I accept my
full share of that blame for not having done something
about it years ago. But Saint Francis himself may have
contributed to the failure of his name and fame being
spread to all corners of the world. For the rules of conduct
promulgated by him for the Minimi were so strict that then

Pope Sixtus IV, although having much admiration for Friar Francis, withheld his approval of them, considering the lifestyle and fasting required for joining the Order much too rigorous for a young man to undertake. (The rules were subsequently approved by a successor Pope.) Thus, the humility and self-effacement he practiced and demanded of his followers may be responsible in large part for his not being better known. The purpose of this little book is to help offset that situation—to introduce English readers to this great man of God, for their own inspiration and edification and for the honor which it will bring to our heavenly Father and to His servant, Saint Francis of Paola.

We find in Saint Francis' life no evidence during his ninety-one years on earth that God denied this devoted son anything for which he had prayed. God so loved His humble servant that whatever Francis asked of Him the Almighty granted. I hope and pray that Saint Francis of Paola in Heaven has a kind and guiding word for all of us who venerate his memory on earth, for I am certain that his word will carry with it the approval and blessing of Almighty God.

Mario M. Segreti
September 8, 1976
Nativity of the Blessed Virgin Mary

Chapter 1

EARLY LIFE OF FRANCIS

The great English poet William Cowper wrote some 200 years ago, "God moves in a mysterious way, His wonders to perform." Christian history is replete with examples of the truth of this aphorism.

The birth of Christ, the Son of God, in a stable in the remote village of Bethlehem, in much despised Judea, some 2,000 years ago, is the outstanding example of Cowper's statement. The appearance of bands of angels singing celestial hymns on the night of the Savior's birth, the unique Star in the sky that guided the Three Kings of the Orient from far away countries to the stable in which the Christ Child lay are historical illustrations of the strange and mysterious ways that God works "His wonders to perform."

No less mysterious and incredible was the instantaneous conversion on the road to Damascus of Saul, the zealous persecutor of the followers of Christ, who of course became St. Paul, the most dedicated and diligent preacher of Christ's Gospel. In reference to God's mysterious way of getting His work done, one must remember that Paul, who in his anti-Christian days had brought death to scores of Christians, became such a brilliant and effective preacher of the religion he once persecuted that, though he never knew Christ personally, he is considered as one of the Apostles, the "Apostle of the Gentiles."

St. Paul gladly suffered a martyr's death under Emperor Nero in the year 67 for his suddenly acquired faith. None of the Apostles originally selected by Christ achieved his success in spreading the Gospel throughout the pagan world of Greece and Rome. It might almost seem that without St. Paul, Christianity could have remained a minor Jewish religious group.

Another instance of the mysterious ways by which God achieves His ends was the sudden conversion of St. Francis of Assisi from a carousing, wasteful son of a rich merchant of Assisi (who frequently found himself in jail) to the fervent champion of the poor and the despised, accomplishing his mission in abject poverty, barefooted and clothed in a simple brown robe.

Perhaps never was Cowper's maxim more fully illustrated than by the life of St. Francis of Paola, the great thaumaturge [miracle worker] from the northeast coast of Calabria, the forefoot of the Italian boot.

At the time St. Francis came into the world, the Catholic Church was in great turmoil. The year he was born, some seventy-six years before Columbus discovered America, the Catholic Church was in the throes of that deep and embarrassing confusion known in history as the Western Schism. There were three claimants to the Papal throne—Gregory XII, the legitimate Pope in Rome, Benedict XIII, in Avignon, and John XXIII, elected by a group of dissident cardinals at an illegal council held in Pisa.

Nineteen months after St. Francis' birth in distant Calabria, far removed from the deep-seated ecclesiastical and political enmities and rivalries of Western Europe, all the cardinals participating in the Council of Constance, in Switzerland, elected Cardinal Oddone Colonna as Martin V, re-establishing the unity of the Church and the legitimate Papal succession.

There is reason to believe that God, in His mysterious way, may have brought St. Francis into the world at this crucial moment in the history of the Church, coincidental with this epochal reconciliation, to mark the special mission He had for the great Calabrian saint and miracle worker. The numerous conciliatory achievements of St. Francis, along with his many miracles, indicate that God had endowed him with unique powers in this direction.

St. Francis' selection by the Lord to serve Him in a singular way was made manifest even before he was born. Nine months before his birth, neighbors were astonished to see tongues of flames dancing above the humble home of Giacomo and Vienna d'Alessio, a deeply religious couple. The neighbors, highly excited, called out the d'Alessios to see this strange phenomena. The d'Alessios were as puzzled as their neighbors. However, though they wondered at the dancing flame, they felt no fear. They saw it as a sign from God. They both continued going about their usual chores, she as a housewife, and he as a farmer—attending Mass daily and always ready to help neighbors. They were well liked by everyone for their kindness and neighborly concern. They had been married in the year 1400, and after fifteen years they still remained childless, much to their regret and despite their continuing fervent prayer.

On Friday, March 27, 1416, St. Francis was born, bringing great joy to the d'Alessios. They recalled the flame that danced over the roof of their house nine months before and now knew what it meant. It had been a sign from Heaven, and that made their new-born son someone special and unique. Giacomo was from a family that had long resided in Paola, a small town located on the northwest shore of Calabria in the province of Cosenza. The mother came from the nearby town of Fuscaldo, nine kilometers northeast of Paola. The towns were part of the Kingdom of Naples.

Devoted to the worship of St. Francis of Assisi, the d'Alessios were sure that the great Saint of the Poor had been instrumental in answering their prayers. In gratitude to him, they named the boy Francis. Needless to say, their neighbors, who held the d'Alessios in high esteem, both for their piety and their unselfishness, were most happy for the parents. However, they felt a strange awe in looking at the new-born child. There seemed to be a soft, haunting melody playing in the child's bedroom and an air of something holy.

But the parents' great joy over their wonderous child was soon clouded. A month after his birth, the mother discovered an abscess in his left eye. All efforts to cure the condition according to the scientific knowledge of the day were futile. In desperation, the mother wrapped up the child and took him to the nearby church. She knelt before the statue of St. Francis of Assisi, imploring the patron saint of the family to save his namesake from blindness. With tears streaming down her face, Vienna promised that if St. Francis cured him, she would arrange for him to serve one year in the Franciscan monastery of St. Mark in nearby Argentano, wearing the habit and fulfilling the vows of the Minor Order.

She returned home confident that the great Saint had heard her plea and that he would intercede for her on behalf of her baby son. Certain that the Saint would not disappoint her, she made little Francis comfortable in his crib. A few days later the eye was miraculously cured, leaving only a small scar. The d'Alessios were so impressed by this great miracle that they became even more fervent devotees of St. Francis of Assisi, whom they prayed to profoundly during their daily Mass, remembering him also in the Rosary every day.

The young Francis accompanied his parents in their daily devotions and meditations, and when he reached a certain age, in answer to an obvious inner call, became even more devout than his parents. He enjoyed praying and meditating on Christ, the Virgin Mary, and St. Francis far more than going out to play with children of his own age. He used to shut himself in his room so that he could concentrate more on his praying and meditating without outside distractions. Frequently his mother had to insist that he leave the house to get some fresh air and exercise. He would go, telling her that he only did so to please her and that he found meditating in the privacy of his room more satisfying and refreshing.

One freezing winter day he was kneeling bareheaded and lightly clothed before images of Christ and the Virgin, saying his rosary, when his mother admonished him for not wearing at least a covering on his head on such a cold day. The Saint-to-be said: "Would you not expect me to take off my hat if I were in front of the Queen of Naples, no matter how cold it was? Isn't the Queen of Heaven far more important than the Queen of Naples?"

When young Francis meditated, he would interlock his fingers tightly, turn his eyes toward Heaven, and become completely unaware of what was going on about him. During moments of his deepest concentration, his body appeared to glow. He followed an ever more rigorous regimen of fasting and abstinence. On Fridays he insisted on eating only bread and water, and on all other days he would abstain from meat and would drink milk only at his mother's insistence. In abstaining from eating meat, he followed his father, who had subsisted on vegetables and fruit all of his life as part of his devotion to St. Francis of Assisi and from his love for animals.

The morning he became thirteen years old, March 27, 1429, he awoke to find his room suffused in light and St. Francis of Assisi at his bedside. St. Francis said: "Tell your parents that the time has come for you to wear the habit of the Friars Minor for one year as your mother promised when, as a baby, you were cured of an abscess in your left eye."

Francis reported the visit from St. Francis to his mother. In keeping with her well-remembered promise, she took him to the Franciscan Monastery of St. Mark at Argentano, twelve miles northeast of Paola. He was greeted by the superior of the monastery, Father Anthony of Catanzaro, who apparently was expecting him. Father Anthony welcomed the boy and invited his parents to stay overnight.

The next day, after Mass, Father Anthony dressed Francis in the habit of a Friar Minor. He also outlined the Order's vows of poverty, chastity, obedience and humility that all had to live by while in the monastery. Francis gladly agreed. He then warmly embraced his parents and watched them leave for Paola quite pleased over having fulfilled their promise to St. Francis.

Francis' religious zeal, his eagerness to help, and the conscientious way in which he performed all assignments deeply impressed the members of the community. He always carried out his work cheerfully and eagerly—whether in the kitchen, in the infirmary, on charitable missions to the poor people in the area, or in gathering wood from the forests that surrounded the monastery. He never complained and seemed never to tire. Always he thanked God for having granted this wonderful opportunity to serve Him, St. Francis, and the people in the area. During this time, he gave his whole attention to learning to read and write. Without neglecting his chores, he also concentrated on studying, especially the Bible and the writings of St. Francis of Assisi. He meditated on what he read and on its application to a life of service to God and mankind. He soon dedicated himself completely to the rigors of an ascetical life. The friars, young and old, were amazed that one so young could so fully commit himself to God. Father Anthony, impressed with his young charge's enthusiasm and devotion, nevertheless had to caution him from time to time for fasting so severely and for not getting sufficient sleep in his zealous concern for prayer, meditation and work. Francis insisted on sleeping on the naked ground, instead of on the thin pallets that the other monks used.

At least three miracles occurred during his year at St. Mark's. The first was an instance of bilocation (appearing in two places at once). While apparently serving at the altar in the chapel, Francis was seen by monks working simultaneously at his chores in the kitchen.

On another occasion, Francis had been assigned the task of preparing the day's meal. He placed the pot over the fireplace with the vegetables in it and the wood ready underneath. Noting that he had time to visit the chapel for prayer and meditation before lighting the fire, he went in. Lost in the ecstasy of prayer and meditation, he forgot his

assignment until hungry monks, greatly annoyed by his ne-
glect, discovered him deep in prayer. Made aware of his
failure, Francis rushed into the kitchen and made the Sign
of the Cross before the fireplace; it immediately burst into
flame, and seconds later the pot began to boil, to the astonishment of the monks. The food was then served on
time and the monks found it more tasteful than the usual
fare.

The third miracle occurred when he was assisting at
Solemn High Mass. The sacristan realized that the fire to
light the incense burner had not been brought into the
chapel. He asked Francis to fetch it from the kitchen.
Unable to find the receptacle for carrying the burning embers, he picked the embers out of the fireplace with his fingers, placed them in the folds of his tunic and, rushing into
the chapel, placed them in the incense burner. Neither his
tunic nor his fingers were scorched, to the wonderment of
all those who observed the young novice's incredible act.

The story of the three miracles soon became known
throughout the diocese. The people came to the monastery
to observe the young novice with these extraordinary
powers. The bishop of the diocese, Mgr. Luigi Imbriaco, a
Benedictine monk, when advised of Francis' miraculous
acts, came to the monastery to meet him and to determine
for himself the truth of what he had heard. He was soon
convinced of the young man's miraculous powers and returned to talk with him many times, sometimes in his cell
and sometimes in a remote corner of the garden, where
Francis used to retire to lose himself in the ecstasy of his
prayers.

When his year at the monastery ended, the monks tried
to persuade him to join the Order, but he refused because
he felt that he had a special calling in the world outside.
He was grateful to the Franciscans for having taught him
how to read and write and for having helped him understand the Bible, the liturgy, and the Christian beliefs and
obligations.

Back with his parents, Francis persuaded them to go on

a pilgrimage to Assisi, the home of their patron saint. This was in 1430, when he was fourteen years old. When the three pilgrims finally reached Rome, they showed little interest in all the great historic monuments and ruins. They were more interested in Christain shrines, particularly the Tomb of St. Peter, where they spent some time renewing their vows and dedication to the Savior, the Virgin Mary, and St. Peter. Wandering the streets of Rome, Francis was deeply disturbed when a cardinal, in flaming red robes, drove by in a gold encrusted carriage, followed by a large retinue of horsemen in bright uniforms. He felt that this was not in keeping with the humble guise of the Savior and his disciples. He could not resist shouting: "The apostles of Jesus Christ did not travel the ways with so much pomp." The cardinal, reputed to have been Giuliano Cesarini, who received his red hat from Martin V in 1426, heard the young man's words, stopped the carriage, and, noting that the young man seemed to be thoroughly sincere in his feelings, said to him: "My son, do not be scandalized by this finery. If we did with less in these times, the dignity of churchmen would be lowered in the eyes of believers, and it would make the worldly despise them." Cardinal Cesarini died in battle against the Turks in 1444.

Arriving in Assisi, in the Umbria region, the d'Alessio family made their first stop the chapel of St. Mary of the Angels, where St. Francis of Assisi first saw the Virgin Mary. Here St. Francis of Assisi had vowed eternal chastity and a life of poverty and piety. Then they visited the basilica dedicated to St. Francis of Assisi. The parents, though pleased to have worshipped in the home shrines of their patron saint, were more pleased in seeing that their son appeared to gain so much inspiration and pleasure from the sites made holy by Il Poverello, the great Saint of the Poor.

Evidently the visit to Assisi and the various shrines dedicated to St. Francis had a profound effect on young Francis. It had convinced him of the life he wanted to live, a

life of extreme self-denial and dedication to the service of
God and the poor. The pilgrimage to Assisi had removed
all doubts from his mind. He returned to Paola, and
though still only fourteen years old, was a fully matured
man of God who had chosen his mission in life. Back on
his native soil, he refused to return to the home of his
parents. He became a hermit. He found a dilapidated barn
roofed over with branches in a remote wooded area a mile
outside Paola, and there he spent his time in prayer, meditation, and study, living on a meager diet of fruit and vegetables. His parents understood and made no objections.
Occasionally they brought him food his mother had prepared according to his rigid rules of abstinence. He was always a dutiful son and was glad to see his parents happy
and in good health, but he preferred the solitude of his
spiritual retreat.

Chapter 2

THE YOUNG HERMIT

Francis was happy in the quietness of his branch-covered barn until the curious began to interfere with his solitude and contemplation. As the number grew and became a continuous distraction, Francis gathered up his books and religious items and followed a stream that ran out of the remote depths of a forest until, at the foot of some mountains, he reached a cave whose entrance was completely hidden by shrubs and vines. He took good care to see that the shrubbery remained as he had found it so he could guard himself from visitors, even though most were motivated by admiration and awe rather than idle curiosity.

With a worn-out shovel he enlarged the cave so that it would stay dry and would give him room for his books, clothes, and holy reminders, and provide a minimum of comfort. The cave, which still exists, is known today as the "Grotto of Penance."

Like St. Francis of Assisi, the young hermit was fascinated by the sights and sounds of birds and insects and of forest animals that roamed the area and drank from the stream that flowed near the cave. The sound of the rain falling through the trees and the rustling of the leaves in the wind gave him a feeling of comfort and companionship. According to his reports, he was continually tempted by the devil, whose blandishments he scorned; in compensation he received visits from angels, who talked to him and entertained him with divine songs. He slept on his hairy cloak, using the stone on which he sat as a headrest. He lived off the vegetation that grew wild and abundantly along the stream and near the cave. This was supplemented by prepared food from his parents and devotees, who visited him from time to time.

Early each morning he apparently walked several miles to attend Mass at the family parish church, the Church of the Virgin of the Mountains, where he had been baptized. Making his breakfast on the fruit along the way, he would return to his cave to pray and meditate for hours on end, losing himself in ecstasy.

Later, in describing his repeated battles with the devil (who submitted him to all the temptations of the world), he said: "The devil, my brothers, believe me, has a consuming hatred against the servants of Christ. The malignant one, seeing that he cannot steal their souls, vents his most terrible wrath on them, forcing them to resist every type of suffering."

One day a young goat, chased by hunters, sought shelter in his cave. The hunters were startled to see a ragged hermit holding their presumed prey in his arms. Deeply shaken by the sight, they called off their dogs (who also seemed to have sensed an unusual situation) and returned to their homes, where they told of their unexpected experience. Soon, many devout people with problems came to visit him, begging his counsel and blessing. The episode of the young goat and the hunters occurred some five years after he started living in his remote cave. He accepted the appearance of the goat and the hunters as a sign from God that it was now time for him to carry out his mission in the world of men.

As a first step in this new phase of his work for God (which was in the year 1435, when he was nineteen years old) and with the help of his devoted parents, he built a cell of stone on a remote part of their farm on the outskirts of Paola. It was located so that it was accessible to those who seriously sought spiritual counsel and encouragement from him. Among his visitors were three men who wanted to join him, adopt his ways, and share in his prayers and penance. Francis realized that this was the next step in ful-

filling his mission, the creation of a religious group. With
the approval of the ordinary of Cosenza, he arranged to
build a chapel and three cells on his parents' property,
adjacent to his cell. He called his small band the "Penitent
Hermits," but the townspeople preferred to call them the
"Hermits of Fra Francesco." His disciples wore simple
brown robes made like a sack, tied around the waist with
rope, with holes for their arms.

The first of these disciples was Fra Fiorentino, a towns-
man of the Saint-to-be, who lived many years in pious self-
denial, doing deeds of charity. The second, Fra Angelo
Alipatti, was a native of Saracena, near Castrovillari,
some thirty miles north of Paola. The third was Fra Nicola
de San Lucido, a few miles south of Paola. He became a
"Blessed." Francis insisted that he and his companions
were lay religious, committed completely to prayer and
charity. A hood, which, it was claimed, was given to St.
Francis by an angel, was added to the sackcloth tunic. The
original hood is still preserved among the effects of the
Saint. All, of course, went about their work in their bare
feet, regardless of the weather.

The three hermits faithfully followed Francis' schedule,
gathering in the chapel several times each day and night to
pray together and to perform simple religious functions,
then retiring, each to his own cell, for further prayer and
meditation. They ate a very simple diet consisting of
bread, legumes, and greens, the latter of which were
gathered from the land or provided by devoted neighbors
and admirers. The rigorous life they lived attracted an ever
increasing number of people, deeply impressed by how
happy the four were in their life of poverty and dedication
to God and prayer. More men came to join the group. This
made Francis very happy, recognizing it as a fulfillment of
his chosen mission. It soon was evident that he had to erect
a monastery.

The Saint designed the monastery according to what he
considered the size needed and the means available. When
the walls were started, a figure, dressed in the habit of a

Friar Minor, appeared from nowhere. The apparition approached Francis and said: "Brother, why are you building a monastery of such limited dimensions to serve and honor the infinite majesty of Him on High?" Francis replied: "How can I do more when I must depend upon the generosity of the faithful?" "Have faith in Providence," the unknown visitor told him. "Demolish what you have built, and rebuild according to the plan that I will trace for you." Having thus spoken, the stranger, with the lay friars watching, traced on the ground a far larger building design. When he had completed his work, he disappeared. Though there was some confusion as to who the apparition might have been, it was obvious that he had been a messenger from Heaven, apparently St. Francis of Assisi. This conclusion was accepted by Pope Leo X in his edict of canonization of St. Francis of Paola.

A few days after the appearance of the strange Friar Minor, Giacomo Tarsia, the wealthy baron of Belmonte and a general in the service of the Venetians, visited the saintly hermit and offered him money and material to build the monastery according to the specifications of the figure from Heaven. Soon, other well-to-do members of the area contributed money and material, while the less fortunate volunteered their handwork, pleased with an opportunity to help the holy man and his followers build a permanent shelter.

During the building of the church, the Saint performed many miracles. The first of these was the removal from the middle of the proposed monastery area of an enormous stone which the workers found impossible to move. When Francis noted their inability to budge it, he ordered them to back away. Then kneeling down and raising his arms, he said a fervent prayer. The gigantic stone raised itself out of the ground, and was easily rolled away to a place where it can be seen today.

On another occasion, a huge rock came rolling down the mountainside toward the workers, busy with their tasks. They were unaware of their danger, but Francis, realizing what was happening, raised his hand and shouted, "In the name of Charity, stop!" The giant boulder stopped dead in its track.

Being in need of food, the workmen caught and slaughtered Francis' pet lamb, Martinello, roasting it in their lime kiln. They were eating when the the Saint approached them, looking for his lamb. They told him they had eaten it, having no other food. He asked what they had done with the fleece and the bones. They told him they had thrown them into the furnace. Francis walked over to the furnace, looked into the fire and called "Martinello, come out!" The lamb jumped out, completely untouched, bleating happily on seeing his master.

When the workers complained that they had to go so far for drinking water, the Saint, praying, struck the ground with a stick, and immediately water gushed out of the ground. The spring still exists and is called the "Cucchiarella."

Francis had a favorite trout that he called "Antonella." One day one of the priests, who provided religious services, saw the trout swimming about in his pool. To him it was just a delicious dish, so he caught it and took it home, tossing it into the frying pan. Francis missed "Antonella" and realized what had happened. He asked one of his followers to go to the priest to get it back. The priest, annoyed by this great concern for a mere fish, threw the cooked trout on the ground, shattering it into several pieces. The hermit sent by Francis gathered up the broken pieces in his hands and brought them back to Francis. Francis placed the pieces back in the pool and, looking up to Heaven, praying, said: "Antonella, in the name of Charity, return to life." The trout immediately became whole and swam joyously around his pool as if nothing had happened. The friars and the workers who witnessed this miracle were deeply impressed at the Saint's amazing powers.

A nobleman of San Lucido, Giovanni di Franco, volunteered to help carry some large stones to the site where they were to be used. Francis gladly accepted his offer and selected a stone which usually took four workers to carry. He made the Sign of the Cross over it, then he picked it up without great effort and placed it on the nobleman's shoulder. The nobleman, who had prepared himself for a crushing load, was stunned by the lightness of the stone and easily carried it to where it was needed.

On another occasion, there was a stone column on the beach that Francis wanted to have brought to the work site. Nicola Piccardi, a gentleman of Paola, agreed to help get the column to where it was needed but said it would require the service of a cart. The holy man said that that was not necessary. He told him: "Don't worry, brother, you can easily carry it by yourself." The puzzled Nicola obeyed. He found the column very light. He placed it under his arm and without strain delivered it to the workers, who were amazed at the ease with which he carried it. The Saint repeated miracles of this kind many times, to the wonderment and awe of numerous observers. Even well-to-do women of the area cheerfully offered their services with some of the heavy work and helped provide food for the workers.

In the forest of Guardia, a town about twelve miles from Paola, there was a number of trees that had been cut down for building the monastery. The Holy Man, with a group of workers, came to the forest in a boat, figuring that it would be easier to transport them by water. One of the trees was so long and heavy that all of the workers together could not drag it to the boat. Francis told them to rest and eat their lunch. When they returned, they found the log on the boat. Astounded, they asked Francis for an explanation. He smiled and told them: "Do not be so amazed, brothers, for it is only proof of the grace of God."

He performed many miracles during the building of this first monastery. One of the most memorable concerned a beam which fell on one of the workmen, crushing him. The Saint knelt beside the mutilated corpse, turned his eyes heavenward, and prayed fervently. He then arose, gathered certain special herbs, and touched certain parts of the mangled body. Then he stepped back, waved his hands, and the man arose from the ground, whole, as if he had only been asleep and was no worse for his experience.

Equally remarkable was the restoration to life of a worker named Domenico Sapio, who had been crushed when a huge pine fell on him. Francis got down on his knees beside the corpse, raised his arms toward the sky and then arose saying: "In the name of Charity, Domenico, Arise!" Domenico arose, dusted himself off, thanked the Saint, and went back to work.

The miracles became so commonplace that the workers and volunteers from the nearby towns and Francis' fellow monks went about their tasks with great unconcern, believing they were under a special protection while they were helping build this monastery to be dedicated to the d'Alessio family patron, St. Francis of Assisi.

When the monastery was finally finished, Francis entered while the workers and monks were outside eating their lunch and, kneeling at the newly built altar, lost himself in prayer. Soon he was transported into ecstasy, and started to shout: "O God of charity! O God of charity!" Three of his monks, who were in the sacristy, heard his ecstatic cry and rushed to the altar to see what was happening. They saw Francis' head crowned with three glittering halos one above the other in the form of a tiara. They fell to their knees in prayer. When he came out of his trance, he went about his work thoroughly refreshed and happy, though he had not eaten his noonday meal.

Perhaps the most amazing of all the miracles during the building of this monastery was one of the first, related to the furnace built to prepare lime for mortar. Shortly after it was completed, workers noticed that some of the stones making up the wall had come loose, either from faulty construction or from the tremendous heat of the fire. Alarmed, the workmen tending the furnace ran to tell Francis, expressing fear that the furnace would collapse. Francis examined the damage and advised the workers to be of good spirit and to trust in the help of God. When all the workers had left for lunch, Francis stood in front of the furnace entrance, lifted his arms in prayer, made the Sign of the Cross over it, then entered into the roaring flames. He assessed the condition of the furnace, then calmly walked back out, his clothes completely unharmed by the fire. The furnace's imperfections were repaired instantaneously.

The furnace is still standing alongside the monastery on the outskirts of Paola, not far from the chapel of St. Mary of the Angels, the first shrine built by St. Francis. This was the furnace from which the Saint later called back to life his pet lamb Martinello, made whole from the fleece and bones thrown into it after the workers had roasted and eaten it. The incident of the burning furnace was attested to by eight different witnesses at the canonization hearings in 1519. All other miracles mentioned were also testifed to by many witnesses at the canonization hearings.

Chapter 3

MORE EARLY MIRACLES

Besides performing the numerous miracles relating to the building of his first monastery, Francis used his amazing miraculous powers on many other occasions as well.

Giacomo di Tarsia, the devout baron of nearby Belmonte, who was first with a generous offer of money and material to build the larger monastery proposed by the apparition of St. Francis of Assisi, developed an abscess on his leg that gravely impeded his movements. The abscess was daily growing worse. The baron's doctors declared the infection beyond cure and indicated that it would ultimately cause the loss of the baron's leg. The baron, who had long known about the miraculous cures by the Saint, finally decided to visit him, with the hope that he might be able to cure him. Accompanied by his wife and many friends and servants, he presented himself to the Saint. Francis, recalling his great and timely contribution for the building of the monastery, greeted him with great warmth. After he had listened to the reason for the baron's unexpected visit, Francis sent one of the monks to his vegetable garden to pick some blades of a grass known as *"unghia cavallina"* ("horse's toenail"). In the meantime, Francis went into the chapel, and kneeling before the crucifix, he bowed his head in prayer. He returned to the baron, sprinkled some powder on the abscess, then placed three blades of the grass across the festering wound. He then bandaged it and told the baron to go home, that his leg would be cured. A few miles outside of Paola, on their way back to Belmonte, the baron turned to his wife, and said: "Giovanna, I no longer feel pain in my leg." He dismounted from his horse, walked around on his leg and found he had been completely cured.

Sometime later, the baron's young son, Galeazzo, developed an illness that rendered him helpless and unable to speak. It was a condition that completely baffled the physicians. After five days of watching his son grow steadily worse, the baron decided to call once again on the Saint of Paola. He sent his steward, Francesco di Marco, to implore Francis to help cure his son. The Saint told the steward to have faith in the goodness of the Creator. He then retired to his cell and prayed with deep devotion. A short while later, the Saint reappeared and in a cheerful voice told di Marco to return to his master and assure him that the child would be made well again. He gave the steward two biscuits and two roots for the boy to eat while prayers of thanksgiving were being said. But before the steward reached the castle, he was met by a servant who told him that Galeazzo had been cured, apparently at the hour the Saint had completed his supplication to God.

Tommasso Piscione, a lawyer in Paola, related another cure by Francis. While going through his church one day, Francis found a boy, a girl, and their mother kneeling before the crucifix, weeping and praying with great fervor. He asked them why they were so distressed. The boy, between sobs, told the Saint that his father was dying of an unknown disease. Deeply moved, Francis put his hand on the boy's head and asked: "Do you know the *"Pater Noster?"* "Not yet," the boy replied, "but I do know the *"Ave Maria."* "Then kneel and recite it," the Saint told him and the little girl who stood beside him. When the children completed the recitation, he gave the boy two biscuits and some fruit, and told him to take them to his dying father, certain that the Virgin Mary would grant him back his health. The boy ran happily to the bedside of his father who, though he had not been able even to drink water for some days, ate the biscuits and fruit. Shortly thereafter he was able to get out of his bed. Three days later he was back at work.

At that time there lived in Cosenza a certain Marcello Cardilla, well known and well liked by people in that area. Two years before he had suffered a stroke that left him paralyzed. He was also covered with leprosy sores that the doctors had declared incurable. Unable to use his hands and feet, and finding it increasingly difficult to speak, the unfortunate had resigned himself to his fate, looking forward to death as relief from his sufferings. Seeing him reduced to such a state, his relatives, according to the testimony at the canonization hearings, decided to transport him to the convent at Paola. Francis was overcome with compassion on seeing the unfortunate man. Without saying a word, the Saint dropped to his knees in deep prayer. When he had finished, he arose, took Marcello by the hand and said: "Brother, in the name of Charity, arise and walk!" At this request, the helpless one snapped out of his lethargy and, while his relatives watched in wonder and awe, arose fully cured.

Francis restored the hearing of many deaf mutes in his section of Calabria. One of the first among these was the boy, Bartolo di Scigliano, who had been deaf and dumb from birth. His parents, having heard of the many great cures performed by the Holy Man of Paola, decided to bring him to the Saint. When Francis saw the handicapped youngster, he clasped his hands together, turned his eyes to Heaven and, after a few minutes of prayer, told the youngster: "My son, repeat after me, 'Jesus, Jesus, Jesus.' " The boy, to the astonishment of all those watching, repeated immediately the name of Jesus three times with absolute clarity.

In the same way Francis cured a twelve-year-old girl, a native of Celico, who also was a deaf mute. After having prayed over her, he made the Sign of the Cross over her lips and said: "My child, in the name of Charity, invoke the name of Jesus in a loud voice." She understood him, called out the name of Jesus and was immediately cured.

He rendered miraculous restorations of sight to numerous blind people, either with a simple Sign of the Cross, the application of certain herbs, a piece of wax, or with holy water. Somehow he made each miraculous cure slightly different, but always with the same results. For instance, Giulia Catalano was born blind. She was seventeen years old when her father, Antonio Catalano, decided to take her to Francis. When they reached the monastery, according to Giovanni Petruccio, they found the Saint busy working his garden, with a bunch of herbs that he had picked in his hand. He took one of the herbs, blessed it and applied it to Giulia's sightless eyes. When he removed his fingers the herb fell to the ground and the girl's sight was restored. This occurred at the Monastery of Paterno.

A man of Amantea had lost his vision seven years before. All efforts to restore it had been in vain. His relatives decided to take him to see the Saint at Paola. According to Giordano Carincella, a friend, Francis comforted the blind man and told him to have faith in the goodness of the Lord. He then made the Sign of the Cross over him and told him to enter into the church to hear Mass. The sightless one obeyed him promptly. At the Elevation of the Host, the blind man cried aloud: "Thank you, O Lord, for your kindness to me. I can see! I can see the Sacred Host!"

He also restored the minds of the mentally deranged and feebleminded, many of whom had suffered their incapacity for years. He also liberated people possessed by demons. For example, one day a possessed woman, Tocca Angitola, was brought by her friends and relatives to the monastery at Paola. They were accompanied by many neighbors, who came to see what would happen. When she neared the Saint, she screamed: "Here is my enemy!" Francis was taken back by the woman's frenzied shouting and ordered further action deferred until the next morning. He then retired to his cell. The next morning, the priest who had been put in charge of caring for the wretched woman began the ceremony of exorcism, with no indication of success. "I have no fear of any of you," she kept screaming. "The only one I fear is Fra Francesco." Francis, who had been calmly waiting in the sanctuary, then came out and approached the woman. He raised his hands in prayer and said: "I command you in the name of God on High to leave the body of this poor creature!" Shaken by the Saint's injunction, the evil spirit replied: "You are in error. I am not a demon. I am the spirit of a venal woman who died twenty-five years ago!" Knowing that this was false, Francis said: "Be silent and obey in the name of the Creator!" The enraged demon threw the woman into body-wracking convulsions until she fainted. A few minutes later she arose, free of the demon and in full possession of her senses, grateful to be free from her torment. She returned to her hometown, a new person.

There was a youth who also was possessed and had been exorcised many times but had never been freed completely from his curse. He refused to go voluntarily to Francis. His parents, with great difficulty, managed to drag him to the monastery. At the sight of the Saint, the youth began shouting and cursing him, calling him a bearded miser, a dirty bundle of rags and chewer of roots. "But who are you?" the Saint asked, showing no annoyance. "We are a legion of demons who live on a hill in the guise of crows. We want to control all of Italy, but we cannot be successful because of you and your powers." The Saint interrupted them and ordered them: "Keep quiet, O treacherous ones, and return to the regions of your punishment." From that moment on the youth was normal, never again bothered by demons.

A young mother gave birth to a boy, but the young parents' happiness was turned to horror when they discovered that their child was born without eyes and with a horribly deformed face. The father, accompanied by Francesco Orbio, a neighbor who later testified to the incident, brought the child to the Saint. Francis told the father to have faith, that God would console him. He dropped to his knees and raised his arms to God in prayer. He then arose, wetted the index finger of his right hand, and tracing on the distorted face the area where the eyes should have been, he said: "In the name of Charity, little brother, open your eyes." Immediately two eyes appeared and opened wide in wonder. He then drew the outlines of a mouth, and the child smiled happily. As the Saint proceeded to trace the other features on the face, they appeared, as if by magic. Soon a normal, symmetrical face of great sweetness and beauty came into being.

The restoration of dead people back to life was the most impressive of Francis' many miracles. In his early years he restored three at Paola alone. We have already discussed how he restored the young man who had been crushed by a beam during the building of the monastery at Paola, and later how he restored the worker who had been crushed to death by a falling pine. But the most remarkable such action involved his favorite nephew, Nicola, the oldest son of his sister, Brigida. Nicola wanted to become one of the followers of his uncle, but his mother objected strenuously. She was adamant. She refused to listen to Francis' pleadings to let her son choose his desired way of life. Suddenly Nicola was struck down by some mysterious illness. Daily he grew worse and worse. Brigida, thoroughly alarmed by the desperate condition of her son, hurried weeping to her brother, imploring his aid on her knees. He brushed aside her entreaties telling her bluntly: "Go away, you are not worthy of being heard by God. You have provoked His anger by your stubborn opposition to His will." Stunned by her brother's rebuke, Brigida returned home in despair to her dying son. Shortly after, her son expired and the body was brought to Francis' monastery for funeral services. The funeral rites ended in late afternoon and the monks began to prepare the casket for burial when the Saint asked everyone to leave the church. When alone, he picked up the body and carried it to his cell. The next day he re-entered the Church and saw his sister prostrated in prayer and grief at the altar. He approached her and said: "If your son should return to life, would you consent to his becoming a religious?" Her eyes lit up with hope as she looked at him, clothed in his sackcloth, and cried: "If Heaven wants it, it will be my greatest consolation!"

Without further word, the Saint returned to his cell and shortly thereafter came out with Nicola, completely recovered and dressed in the simple habit of a monk. He was greeted with joy by all the relatives and friends who had followed his mother into the church. The Saint advised his followers that his miracles had to be consistent with the will of God.

All of these miracles were attested to under oath by numerous witnesses before the bishop of the Cosenza diocese, and later during the canonization hearings in Rome in the spring of 1519.

Chapter 4

CALABRIAN WORKS

The stories of Francis' many miracles spread like wild-fire throughout Calabria, and the natives of that region of Italy sought out the Saint to beg him to demonstrate his divine powers in their communities.

From Spezzano, one of the more populous cities in the province of Cosenza, some twenty-five miles northeast of Paola, came a large delegation, extending an official invitation to come to their city. After two years, the earnest entreaties of the citizens of Spezzano broke down Francis' hesitation, and he agreed to accompany them to their city.

His visit to Spezzano took place in 1456, after he had received proper clearance from the archbishop, Monsignor Pirro Caracciolo, successor as head of the archdiocese to his Uncle Bernardino. When Francis reached the town and had had an opportunity to appraise it, he realized the appropriateness of building here the third monastery of the Minimi (the name the Order had selected). The civil authorities were pleased to hear of his plans and offered all possible assistance to him.

Francis, after careful study, selected a site that offered the necessary privacy for his monks, but would still make the church readily accessible to the people, who regarded him with such deep veneration and wonder. The monastery was completed in several years, and he dedicated it to the Holy Trinity.

In the course of building this third monastery, Francis was also called upon to perform several miracles. Two young workers were carrying a huge beam when it slipped and fractured the leg of one. The Saint made the Sign of the Cross, and the leg was made whole again, to the amazement of the onlookers.

Another miracle was reminiscent of one he had performed during the building of the first monastery, in Paola. The workers found that there was no drinking water near the building site. When the Saint was informed of this, he came to the site and touched a large stone, out of which sprung a stream of water that is still flowing.

People who were handicapped, in ill health, or spiritually disturbed came daily into Spezzano from the surrounding towns to see him. They were not only from the working class but also from the well-to-do and the nobility. Francis helped them all, always in the name of *Caritas*—Charity.

One day a rich, young nobleman named Gregory, who had suffered a long time from dropsy, came to the Saint from the small town of Trebisacce. He appeared before him along with other sufferers and, weeping, begged the Servant of God to help him. He said that if he could be cured he would gladly become a member of his Order. The Saint, deeply moved by the young man's tears and intention, assured him that God would remove his affliction. He then took him by the hand and made the Sign of the Cross over him. The young nobleman was siezed with a terrible fit of coughing, which caused him to expel much phlegm. In a few moments his body was completely normal and he had regained full possession of himself. The grateful young man threw himself down before the Saint and tried to kiss his feet. The Saint would not permit him to do this, lifting him up and telling him that he should thank God, not him, for this recovery. True to his promise to the Saint, the young man immediately asked to be made a member of the Order and, upon induction, served with great piety and dedication, dying at a very old age.

It was during the great famine, which had created wide desolation and misery in Calabria, that the presence of the Saint was found most consoling and fortunate. The people, largely tillers of the soil, whose fields had been producing fewer and fewer crops, were starving to death and viewing the future with hopelessness. Many families were without anything to eat. They were condemned to listen to weeping children begging for bread, without the slightest chance of satisfying their need. Most of the neighbors were in the same situation. There was only one man in Spezzano who could help them, Francis of Paola.

No one who came to him was turned away empty-handed. One day three individuals were found lying along the side of the road, where they had fallen from hunger. They were at the point of dying. Francis was called. He hurried over, pulled out a crust of bread from his tunic, blessed it and fed it to the unfortunates. Immediately they revived and, after thanking their benefactor, went on about their business.

The monastery was daily besieged by people begging for food. They were not only from Spezzano but from surrounding towns where the Saint's prodigies had been heard of. A few made arrogant demands that he fulfill their needs completely. Francis listened patiently and sympathetically and satisfied their needs without acceding to exorbitant demands. When the arrogant ones received his bounty, they seemed to understand why he could not have given them more and showed proper appreciation. To some he would give a piece of bread, to others a handful of flour or a portion of cooked beans or vegetables, and to some fruit, all of which were miraculously sufficient to fill the needs of the people involved.

Whenever the supply of food seemed to be near exhaustion, he went into the church and prayed fervently, and soon the trees, fields and gardens would flourish, and he was able to continue his distribution. It was reported at the canonization process that this food was of superior taste and flavor.

The Saint and his followers regularly visited the luckier farmers and the noble and wealthy families, exhorting them in the name of God to share their food with their unlucky neighbors. His fellow monks were so inspired by Francis that their eloquence won the support of some of the most miserly and hard-hearted. In the meantime, the Saint and his followers further mortified themselves, eating less, fasting more often, and praying longer and more fervently to placate the anger of God. The people, noting this further self-sacrifice on the part of Francis and his monks, finally understood that the famine was punishment from Heaven for the selfish, sinful lives they were living. They appreciated the fact that if it had not been for Francis coming into the area and establishing the new monastery, the famine would have been more devastating. In gratitude and repentance, they returned to the churches as regular worshippers, thanking God for sending Francis among them to lead them out of their moral degradation.

At the monastery of the Holy Trinity at Spezzano, two of the friars became famous. One was Giovanni Cadurio, a member of the rich and noble Roccabernarda family from the Catanzaro province. As a young man he had joined the Minimi, but as he grew older, he gave way to the siren call of the outside world and ran away. One day, months later, he came through Spezzano with his lady love. He had to pass in front of the monastery door. Francis, aware of the presence of his fallen-away disciple, instructed the doorkeeper to ask him in and to enclose him in a cell. After he had been locked up for some time, banging on the door and shouting to be let out, Francis came to him. The presence of the Saint calmed him. Francis said to him: "Brother, out of charity, kill the venomous serpent that possesses you." On hearing this, the young man burst into tears, repented his sinful action and asked that he again be clothed in the habit of the penitents. Thereafter he dedicated himself completely to a life of penance, piety and charity, and later was ordained a priest. Francis took him with him to France, but after the death of King Louis XI, he sent him back to Spezzano for having disobeyed one of his orders. After rendering important services to the Minimi, Father Giovanni died in the odor of sanctity in the monastery of Spezzano in 1524.

The other of his followers who is remembered for problems he encountered in becoming a loyal follower of Francis was Bernardino Otranto from Cropalati, in the province of Cosenza. Bernardino as a youth had enrolled in the Order, but his family, which was wealthy and interested in worldly things, forced him to leave. One day Bernardino came to Spezzano and was drawn to the monastery. Francis sensed his presence. The Saint invited him in and placed him in a cell, locking the door. Later he returned and found Bernardino weeping and remorseful, repenting his behavior, begging the Saint to take him back among his religious. Francis welcomed him back.

When word of this reached his family in Cropalati, two of his brothers came to the monastery in Paola, where the Saint had transferred him. They argued so strongly that they finally induced him to return home. But hardly a month had gone by when Bernardino, weeping, presented himself to Francis, again begging him to take him back into the Order. The Man of God, without committing himself, asked him if he would go to Naples and deliver a very important letter to King Ferrante. Bernardino took the assignment enthusiastically and started out for Naples immediately. However, when he returned to Paola, he found his two brothers waiting for him, and they again forced him to return home. Bernardino turned to the Saint, who told him: "Go with them, my son, for your relatives will not prevail. You will ultimately become one of us."

Francis' prophecy was realized. Shortly thereafter, Bernardino left his family home again and returned to the Saint, donning the simple garb of the penitent friars. This time he remained until his death. He became a priest and his humility and devotion so impressed the Saint that he made him his confessor. Francis took him to the French court, and when he found himself dying, named him vicar general of the Minimi. He received the gift of prophecy and predicted the day of his own death at the convent of St. Louis in Naples on October 25, 1520.

Toward the end of 1458, Francis went to Corigliano Calabro on the Gulf of Taranto, where he was invited, by the people of the town and by Count Bernardino Senseverino of Chiaromonte, the Lord of the area, to establish a monastery. His wife was Princess Elenora Piccolomini, of Rossano, through her father grand niece of King Ferdinand II of Naples and through her mother niece of Pope Pius III.

Having observed the wonderful results which the monasteries founded by the Saint produced on localities in which they were built, the Count was anxious to have one in his dominion. Corigliano was a garden spot, noted for its olive groves and flowers. After receiving clearance from the archbishop of Rossano, in whose diocese Corigliano was located, the Saint went to the city, where he was received with great enthusiasm. The whole population, led by the Count, his wife, members of the nobility and the clergy, met him outside the walls and accompanied him to the town's principal church. The old residents could not recall a greater turnout of people and dignitaries or a wilder burst of enthusiasm in welcoming a visitor in the long history of the city. The Count offered the hospitality of his home, but Francis refused and joined his friars in a nearby retreat, more in keeping with their vows and needs. Shortly thereafter he moved to a hut that he had built with his own hands in a wooded valley. This became his home, where he retired to rest and meditate during the day and to study and sleep at night. After the canonization of the Saint, this hut became a shrine, which is still revered by the people of Corigliano.

The ground on which he planned to build this fourth monastery belonged to a certain Luigi Romeo who was deeply pleased that the Saint had selected his land for this purpose. Romeo gladly turned it over without charge to the Saint, and Francis made immediate arrangements to start building his fourth monastery. The townspeople of all stations, including the Count and his family, put themselves at the disposal of the Saint, willing to do whatever he asked of them.

The laying of the cornerstone for the monastery is remembered because of Francis' strange remarks on the occasion. Placing his fingers on the cornerstone, the Saint turned to the people and said: "Brothers, have the locusts ruined your harvests, your vinyards, your olive crops? Have the Turks invaded your land?" They all responded: "No." "Well then remember that the day this stone shall be dishonored, your city will be the victim of these misfortunes." The people felt that the things that the Saint had mentioned could not happen, so they dismissed them, but 138 years later, in 1596, the monastery was taken away from the Minimi and turned over to another order. On the same day that this happened clouds of grasshoppers invaded the Corigliano area, destroying the crops. Public prayers and penitential processions were of no avail; the grasshoppers continued their destruction. Finally, an old resident, Andrea Magrino, recalled the words of Francis at the cornerstone laying in 1458 and advised his fellow townsmen to restore the monastery to the Minimi as quickly as possible. When the Minimi regained possession of the monastery, the cloud of grasshoppers disappeared.

Shortly after this incident a fleet of Saracen galleys, cruising in the Ionian Sea, anchored at Corigliano, and the infidels swarmed into the city. They attacked the monastery of the Minimi, and the monks, in no position to defend themselves, ran away, leaving behind one old friar who was so crippled he was unable to move. The unfortunate monk, hearing the Saracens approaching, prayed to the founder of the monastery. The Saint appeared and told him not to be afraid, for no one would enter to harm him. He placed a cane that he was carrying against the door. Though the invaders rained blows on the door, they were unable to force it open. They soon gave up the effort and joined their companions in attacking the city. The cane, gold plated, has been preserved in the monastery.

The people of the city fought bravely against the Saracens but were forced back steadily until an old man shouted: "Coriglianese, fight on. We are sure to win. St. Francis of Paola has promised to defend our land from the invasion of the infidels." At these words, the besieged, though fewer in number than the invaders and weary with much fighting, suddenly found new strength, rushed upon their foe and soon routed them and forced them to run to their ships, leaving a great number of dead behind. Corigliano had been saved by St. Francis in its most trying hour. In humble gratitude, the people made him the patron saint of the city.

The concern of St. Francis for Corigliano was again demonstrated in 1767 when a terrible earthquake devastated the Calabrian peninsula, sparing Corigliano, which sustained almost no damage. That year, in deep gratitude, the people erected a marble statue to him in front of the monastery chapel.

In the building of this fourth monastery (which went through so many vicissitudes), the Saint performed a number of miracles. It was noted that water for the use of the monastery would have to be carried from some distance away. Francis went to the nearest spring, blessed it, then said: "In the name of Charity, sister, follow me!" At this command the water followed him in a track he traced behind him with a stick, until he reached the monastery, four miles away. Later he arranged for the stream to provide water for three fountains in the city itself. In memory of this miracle, the stream is called the "New Water of St. Francis of Paola."

To make certain that Corigliano would have all the water it needed, the people decided to build an aqueduct. More than 300 workers were engaged in this work. One day at lunch time, two of the noblemen that were helping were brought two "focacce," flat, round loaves of bread. They began to eat one while the workers, having no food, watched them. Francis came to them saying: "Brothers, you have done right to restore your strength, but it is also necessary to restore the strength of the others, because the grace of God must be extended to all." He then took the second loaf from them, blessed it and distributed it among the other workers, all of whom were amply satisfied.

Though Francis was concerned with the building of monasteries to house more followers of his order, he was also concerned with helping lay people reform their lives and become true Christians. While deep in prayer in the church at Corigliano, he was approached by a woman who had left her husband some eighteen years before, had never been to church since, and had lived a life of sin. She approached the Saint and recited her sinful ways and her fear for the punishment of God. She dropped to her knees and asked for Francis' help. The Saint blessed her. When she arose, weeping, she told the Saint how she hated her past life. She returned to God and thereafter lived a life of penance and prayer.

When Francis visited Spezzano in 1460, he received a request from the people of Crotone to come to their city and erect a monastery. He was so preoccupied with other things that he decided to turn the task over to Father Paolo Rendacio, then in charge of the monastery at Paterno. Father Rendacio went to Crotone, won the respect and trust of the authorities there, and built the fifth Minimi monastery, which was named the Monastery of Jesus and Mary.

For several years, Francis spent his time traveling from one monastery to another—Paola, Paterno, Spezzano and Corigliano—performing cures and other prodigies. Once, while in Paterno, people who wanted to see him approached the chapel and found him so deep in prayer they decided not to disturb him. When they returned to the street, they were surprised to see him talking to some people. They hurried back into the chapel and saw him still lost in prayer. It was an instance of bilocation, Francis' ability to be in two places at one time.

Chapter 5

FRANCIS IN SICILY

The fame of Francis as a miracle worker and holy man spread throughout lower Italy and Sicily, which had been separated from Naples on the death of King Alfonso V and turned over to John I of the Spanish branch of the House of Aragon.

A Sicilian nobleman, Bernardo Caponi, exiled for political reasons from his city of Milazzo, was living in Paola with another Sicilian nobleman, Francesco Maiorano. He went to the celebrated Saint in hope of getting him to visit Milazzo in Sicily. The Saint prophesied to Bernardo that he would soon be welcomed back to Milazzo, some fifteen miles northwest of Messina. With the change of rulers in 1458, Bernardo returned to Sicily, where he was greeted with great warmth by his townsmen. He described so enthusiastically and with so much sincerity the amazing cures and miracles performed by the Calabrian Holy Man that the town council decided to send two of its leading magistrates to prevail upon Francis to visit Milazzo. After several years had passed, the Saint finally accepted the invitation, seeing it as a message from God to widen the area of his activities beyond Calabria.

In 1464, at the age of forty-eight, he set off for Sicily, accompanied by Father Rendacio and Brother Giovanni di S. Lucido. They followed the northwest coast of Calabria. When they reached Borello Pass, near the Calabrian town of Palmi, they discovered that they had no bread. A committee of nine from the village of Arena, who had come to welcome them, also was without bread. Undaunted, the Saint turned to Nicola Banaro, one of the committee, who protested apologetically that, unfortunately, he also was without bread. The Saint said: "Give me your pouch, I am certain that there is bread in it." He reached into the pouch and, to the bewilderment of all, particularly poor Nicola who could not believe his eyes, pulled out a loaf of hot bread, which appeared as if it had just been taken from the oven. Completely casual, the Saint blessed the bread with the Sign of the Cross and distributed it to the people who had come to greet him. The more he distributed, the more it grew. After all had eaten their fill, marveling at the superb flavor, there was still bread left over, as in the case of the two similar miracles of Christ in the desert. The committee, deeply impressed by the miracle of the bread, reverently followed the Saint and his two companions for two whole days, to Catona, near the place where the ferry to the Sicilian shores was located. On the journey they continued to eat the bread that Francis had produced so miraculously. It continued to be fresh and delicious.

The ferry to Messina left Villa S. Giovanni, about three miles below Catona, and about four miles opposite the Messina lighthouse. The Saint, his two companions and the nine-man committee from Arena arrived at the ferry slip. The Saint approached one of the ferry captains, Pietro Coloso by name, who was preparing to leave with a load of construction lumber for Messina. He saluted Coloso and asked him in a humble voice if, for the love of Jesus Christ, he would be kind enough to transport him and his two companions to the Sicilian shores. Coloso said coldly: "I will be glad to, just as long as you pay me." "But we, dear brother, are asking for your charity because we have no money." "What does that mean to me?" Coloso replied scornfully. "If you do not have money to pay me, I do not have a boat to carry you."

Then occurred what is perhaps the most spectacular and memorable of the Saint's many miracles. Completely undisturbed by the rude rebuff, the Man of God walked down the beach about a stone's throw away, and knelt in prayer for a few seconds. He then arose, blessed the gentle tide washing the beach, and to the astonishment of the people watching, including his two religious companions and the committee of nine from Arena—and, of course, Coloso— he spread his mantle on the waves, picked up one corner with his staff, and holding it up like a sail, proceeded rapidly and calmly across the four mile strait toward Messina. His miraculous action brought shouts of wonder from the watchers, and consternation to Coloso. The ferryman, completely unnerved, shouted to the Saint to come back, that he would be glad to ferry him and his two companions across for nothing. But the Saint sailed on completely unconcerned. Coloso hurried Father Rendacio and Brother Giovanni onto his ferry and set off in pursuit of the Saint, who continued sailing across the treacherous waters of the Strait of Messina, smoothly and without the slightest difficulty.

When St. Francis neared Messina, he saw that there was a large number of people on the shore, watching in astonishment and moving toward the point where he would land. He shifted his direction so that he would reach the shore beyond the lighthouse and a ridge of rocks jutting out far into the water, providing him an isolated spot to land. The place where he landed was called the Holy Sepulchre. In 1503, a Minimi monastery and a church called "Our Lady of the Grotto" were built there to commemorate the Saint's landing site in Sicily.

The ferryman Coloso followed the Saint across the strait and ran to him greatly agitated, begging for forgiveness. The Saint and his two companions, to avoid demonstrations, quickly proceeded on the road to Milazzo, across the northeast edge of Sicily.

When they arrived at a location called "Pond of the Hanged," they found a body dangling from the frame, hanged three days before. The Saint, moved with pity, removed the rope from around the dead man's neck with the help of Brother John and gathered him into his arms. Father Rendacio refused to interfere in a legal execution.

Casting his eyes to Heaven, the Saint said a prayer and the hanged man sprang back to life. The revived criminal fell to his knees at the feet of the Saint, in deep gratitude. He asked of Francis that, having saved his body, he also help save his soul by making him a member of his order. The hanged man, whose name is unknown, lived a long and useful life as a Minimi friar.

On the fourth of April, 1464, they reached Milazzo, a port founded by the Greeks many centuries before the coming of Christ and originally given the name Mylae. The Saint and his companions were greeted with great joy and reverence by the leaders and people of Milazzo, as he had been greeted in cities on the Continent. Similar to other such visits, the Saint refused the hospitality of the nobility and leaders of the city and insisted on living in the building set aside as a public hospital for the poverty-stricken. He visited the unfortunates lodged in the primitive ramshackle center, and he and his companions nursed them and took care of them.

In the meantime the city council, as shown by available municipal records, turned over the Church of St. Blaise and its terrace, including the Gate of King James, to St. Francis. He was pleased by this gift but did not start building a monastery until January 17, 1465, after he had obtained the approval of the archbishop of Messina, Giacomo Tudisco (1450-1474). The permission stipulated that he was to receive not only all the ground necessary but also all else that would be needed to erect the monastery according to his plans. The Saint renamed the church "Jesus and Mary."

The Sicilian historian Francesco Perdichizzi, in *Melazzo Sacra,"* reports that, to keep the foundations firm, the monastery was built on two huge blocks of marble placed in loose, sandy soil. It was enclosed with a cloister wall. The marble blocks had been dug up so that a well could be created for drinking water for the workers. The water was found to be salty. The Saint rendered it potable by making the Sign of the Cross over it, but he warned them, however, that as soon as the monks had built a cistern to catch rain-water, the well would turn salty and undrinkable again. Fourteen years later the Well of Saint Francis, as the natives called it, turned salty. However, it was found that the salt water had curative properties.

One of the beams for the roof was found to be too short. When the Saint was apprised of this, he walked over to the beam, made the Sign of the Cross over it, then stretched the beam to the required length, to the astonishment of the workers and other observers.

Father Perdichizzi records another act of supernatural intervention. The Saint had asked a captain of one of the ships in Milazzo harbor if he, out of charity, would give him one of the ship's bells for his monastery church. The captain refused. The Saint pleaded with him a second and third time, but he still refused. When the captain tried to sail out of the harbor, his ship would not move, despite all the efforts of his crew and the harbor workers. Finally he gave the Saint the bell and his ship sailed away without difficulty. A second bell was donated by the King of Naples.

The new monastery and church were completed within three years. An impressive marble statue of the Virgin Mother and Christ Child was donated by the Ventimiglia di Geraci family. The statue is the object of deep veneration. Even the barbarous Mohammedan seafarers, who occasionally berthed at Milazzo, venerated the statue, according to Father Napoli, a Minimi priest. There are preserved seven letters that the Saint wrote from Sicily to his nobleman friend Simone d'Alimena of Paola, asking him to take care of certain matters relating to the Minimi monasteries in Calabria. The first letter is dated September 29, 1464, and the seventh November 1, 1467.

The Saint's compassionate concern for the poor and the afflicted and his charismatic personal attraction, which brought so many to enroll in his order and fill his monasteries, became the wonder of Sicilians throughout the island. There was a constant stream of visitors anxious to see the Saint and share his blessings.

Many Sicilian cities sent requests to have Minimi cloisters erected within their boundaries so that they too could benefit from the good things the monasteries seemed to bring to a locality. Where monasteries were built, the locality seemed to flourish and prosper.

In early 1468, after three years in Sicily, he returned to his headquarters monastery at Paterno, in Calabria. He continually received requests from many Sicilian towns asking for the establishment of Minimi monasteries in their areas, but the Saint was unable to take advantage of these offers, much as he regretted it, because of too few monks with organizational ability. He never personally returned to Sicily, but through the years the Order established a number of monasteries—near Palermo, Messina, Catania, Syracuse, and other Sicilian cities.

Chapter 6

RETURN TO CALABRIA

On his return to Calabria in 1468, Francis found many ship captains and ferrymen eager to take him back to his native soil. When he reached Catona, on the Calabrian toe, he was greeted with great enthusiasm by the people, who rushed to meet him, shouting: "Here comes the Saint! Here comes the Saint!" Though pleased with the wonderful reception he received, Francis, now fifty-two years of age, without taking time out to rest, worked himself free of the adulating crowd and proceeded alone and on foot to the Minimi monastery in Paterno, some ninety miles away.

When he reached Paterno several days later, he was greeted with solemn ceremony by the townspeople, grateful to have the Miracle Worker back among them again. Needless to say, the monks were overjoyed to have their founder return to resume the direction of the Minimi activities in Calabria. For, in addition to his power to perform miracles, Francis was also a superb organizer, administrator and leader of men; while still fulfilling his other functions, he seemed to have an intuitive understanding of what was needed to promote and enlarge his Minimi operations.

As he moved around to the various monasteries, he continued to heal the sick, to comfort the distressed, and to fill every demand. Everywhere he was enthusiastically received, but he did not let the admiration of the people interfere with his periods of prayer and meditation, or with carrying out his administrative duties.

While the miracles he worked daily were too numerous to be recorded by his biographers, his methods have been noted. Some cures he effected with herbs and leaves from the monasteries' gardens, some with different kinds of beverage, others by sending the sick selected fruit from the monasteries' orchards, including, in one instance, strawberries. According to Gianfrancesco Arena, the twenty-fifth witness at the Saint's canonization inquest in Calabria, he distributed figs, which he had made grow out of season, to produce one cure. He also restored many back to health with the touch of his hands, with certain words, or with a compassionate look—always, of course, in the name of "*Caritas*" (Charity), the key word of his mission.

Bernardino Mello di Castiglione, who had been crippled two years by an abscess on his thigh, finally came to Francis in the hope of being cured. The Saint not only healed his long-standing affliction, but in response to his entreaties, accepted him into the Minimi. For some twenty years Brother Bernardino lived in perfect health without the slightest pain from his terrible ailment. But one day, forgetting the grace he had received, he decided to leave the Minimi and join the Conventual Friars Minor, a Franciscan Order. As soon as he took off his Minimi tunic, the abscess in his leg reopened, and he was in greater pain than before. There is no further record of Bernardino.

Another miraculous cure that attracted wide attention was that of Roberto Borgo di Cosenza. Roberto, married and with children, had made a good living as a copyist of religious books and tracts, a lucrative business in those days when the printing press was still new and very expensive. Suddenly he was attacked by arthritis, which completely crippled his writing arm and hand. For two full years he sought without success from the doctors in his town the means for remedying this disastrous condition. His family suffered greatly from his inability to earn money. Roberto's wife, who had heard of Francis' many miraculous cures, pleaded with him to go to the Holy Man and see if he could cure his right arm. But Roberto, discouraged by the many doctors and remedies he had tried and convinced that his condition was hopeless, brushed aside her pleas. However, she persisted. Finally Roberto, tortured night and day by pain, agreed. They made their way to Paterno, about five miles southwest of Cosenza. They found the Saint resting in the shadows of a giant oak tree. As they approached him, Francis, noting Roberto's crippled right arm, said in a sympathetic tone: "My good brother, you must think of curing your arm because you must copy many more books." His wife pleaded: "Dear father, can you give us a remedy for this condition? Everything we have tried so far has been in vain." Francis said: "It needs simply to be washed."

Duly impressed, the two hurried home. However, when they reached home, they were so exhausted that they went to sleep without doing what the Saint had told them. But the next morning, in spite of the failure to follow the Saint's instructions, the pain had left his arm and he could move it freely. He rushed downstairs and found that his writing ability had returned completely. Overwhelmingly grateful for the cure, Roberto returned to Paterno to thank the Saint. He was greeted cheerfully by Francis, who told him to thank God, not him, and to live the life of a good Christian. Roberto assured him that he would. Thereafter he took much more seriously the religious books he was copying and lived a more spiritual existence.

Ranuccio Parisi, as he himself reported at an inquest on the Saint in Cosenza, had also been severly crippled in both arms by arthritis, incapacitating him completely for several years. No remedies prescribed by his doctors helped him in any way, and his condition was getting worse. Finally he was prevailed upon to visit the Saint at the monastery in Paterno. After greeting him with great tenderness, Francis told him to join him for Mass in the church. After Mass was over, the Saint took him out into the monastery garden where he stripped off some leaves from a plant, saying: "Dear brother, boil these leaves and wash your arms with the water." Ranuccio hurried home and made haste to carry out the Saint's orders. However, he had hardly set the water to boil when the pain in his arms became so excruciating that, in agony, he poured the slightly warm water into a basin and began to wash his arms. As he applied the warm water, the pain disappeared from his arm and never returned, and he was able to resume his regular work.

Francis, though universally venerated, was on occasion subjected to abuses. Two hermits from the environs of Marco d'Ancona, drawn by his great fame, came to Paola to join the Minimi. The Saint, as was his habit, wanted to test their sincerity. After he had interviewed them, he found one truly humble and willing. When the other hermit learned that he had been rejected, he became greatly incensed, cursed the Saint and drew a knife with which he advanced to stab him. Francis looked at him calmly, saying: "In the name of God, stop!" At these words, the would-be killer was frozen into immobility, standing like a statue. The Saint implored him to have a change of heart, but, once released from his spell, the angry hermit spurned Francis' offer and left, hurling insults at him. The Saint sadly watched him leave, unrepentant.

Francis continued to devote himself to his mission of educating and helping the people. Faithful to his commitment to a life of extreme austerity, prayer and meditation, he nevertheless devoted his free time to assisting with community problems and in concern for the welfare of people in every station.

About 1469, at the insistent entreaties of the population, Francis agreed to have a Minimi monastery and church erected in Maida, some thirty miles west of Catanzaro, the provincial capital. The committee that had visited him promised to help in every way feasible so that a Minimi monastery would be built as quickly as possible in their locality. While the Saint was deeply moved by the committee's earnest plea, he had to keep himself free so that he could supervise properly the many monasteries and activities with which he was concerned. One of his most urgent involvements was the erection of a third church in his native town of Paola. He regretted that he himself could not take charge of the building of this new monastery, but he assured the delegation from Maida that he would assign the task to one of his most competent assistants.

Shortly thereafter he dispatched Father Francesco Maiorana, one of the first to join him, to Maida. In ancient times known as Melanium, the city is located on the top of a high hill from whose elevation all of the western end of Calabria, with its rolling meadows and woods, rich with sun and vegetation, can be viewed. On his arrival, Father Maiorana was greeted with great joy and respect, for the Maidans were aware of the high esteem in which the Saint held him. Father Maiorana in a few days quickly and efficiently disposed of preliminary requirements and arrangements and proceeded with the construction of the church and monastery. The church and monastery were to be dedicated to Jesus and Mary. When the construction was well underway, Francis decided to inspect it personally. As expected, he was greeted enthusiastically by the population, who followed him with deep interest and veneration on his tour. The Saint found everything in order. He was deeply pleased by the efficient way in which Father Maiorana had carried out his assignment. The exact date of the Saint's visit to Maida is not known, but it was obviously toward the end of the construction work.

In Paterno, where he had established his headquarters, Francis was not only concerned with the success of existing monasteries and other activities, particularly the recruiting of new members, but also with obtaining an official recognition of his order by the ecclesiastical authorities. Furthermore, he wanted that approval, not because of petitions by influential churchmen, but because of spiritual benefits to the members of the Minimi and also to the people near the monasteries.

According to reports made at the inquest at Cosenza and attested to by Giovanni Antonachio and Salvatore Scano in Paterno, on several occasions he miraculously cooked pots of beans without fire to feed a crowd of hungry workmen. The pots in which these beans were cooked have been preserved in the Minimi monasteries in Paterno and Paola.

Bernardino Pugliano of Paterno attested to another impressive miracle wrought by Francis. One day Pugliano set fire to a stand of trees and shrubs to clear his land so that he could cultivate it. A strong wind arose and caused the flames not only to burn out the trees and shrubbery on his property, but to spread to adjoining fields, threatening stacks of lumber that had been prepared for the building of another Minimi monastery. Francis happened to be nearby and saw the flames sweeping rapidly toward his precious lumber. He raised his hand and shouted: "Fire, in the name of Charity, burn what you are supposed to burn, but do not touch what is mine." Pugliano, who was present and watching helplessly as the flames went out of control, said that at these words the fire stopped and smouldered out. The Saint's lumber remained untouched.

The stories of the Saint's incredible and continuous miracles, plus his power to draw followers to a life of self-mortification, prayer, and unselfish commitment to the service of their fellowmen, spread like wildfire throughout Italy, creating great interest in both secular and ecclesiastical circles. The Vatican, despite the many conflicts that were going on in Europe and the devastation caused by the Turks to Eastern European and Balkan nations, became aware of Francis' extraordinary achievements.

Chapter 7

THE POPE INVESTIGATES

In 1464, on the death of Pius II, a Venetian, Pietro Barbo, succeeded to the Papal throne under the name of Paul II. Though publicly he approved and promoted the magnificence of the Renaissance, he personally lived a very simple and humble life. Upon his elevation to Pope, he immediately gave thought toward reforming the religious and moral attitudes of the times, particularly among the clerics. Though he was not able to prevent all excesses, Paul II greatly tightened the lax moral behavior of most of the clergy and his lay officials.

However, it was the threat from the Turks that concerned him most, as they devastated Christian cities and churches in Eastern Europe. The conquered cities and nations pleaded for the Pope's intervention. In addition, the King of Bohemia, who had adopted a heresy, was trying to banish all Catholic clergy from his kingdom. King Mathias of Hungary, in support of the Pope, defeated the Bohemian king and restored Bohemia to the Catholic faith. Pope Paul II adhered strictly to proper procedures in the appointment of ecclesiastical officials, condemned acts of simony, and punished severely the Fraticelli, "Little Brothers," who were preaching heretical doctrines in the area of Ancona and in parts of Germany. He also effected major reforms in the monasteries, and forced closer observance of monastic discipline.

Paul II, despite many more pressing problems, also decided to investigate the activities of Francis of Paola, whose miraculous cures, strict code of living, and growing number of followers and monasteries had attracted wide European interest.

It may have been that Monsignor Pirro Caracciolo, archbishop of Paola, had written to Pope Paul II requesting Papal approval for the Saint and his devout hermit friars, in gratitude for the wonderful work they had done in Calabria and Sicily. Anyway, the Pope in his zeal for the good of the Church and the saving of souls, decided to send a personal envoy to report on this miracle worker who was becoming a Catholic legend. He named one of his most trusted chamberlains, Monsignor Girolamo Adorno, a noble Genoese, to make the investigation and report back his findings directly to him.

Monsignor Adorno, armed with letters from Pope Paul II to the archbishop of Cosenza, left Rome and journeyed to San Lucido, just outside Paola, where Archbishop Caracciolo was staying at that time. Archbishop Caracciolo received the Papal delegate with great respect and honor, meeting him on the outskirts of San Lucido with all his priests and the nobles and leaders of the community and escorting him to his residence.

The Papal representative spent a few days at the chancery, recovering from his long journey from Rome, asking many questions about Francis, the miracles he had wrought, the followers he had attracted, and the monasteries he had built. Archbishop Caracciolo, with great enthusiasm, recounted the many wonderful facts about the miracle-working Hermit: his many good deeds in the name of Charity, his many miracles—curing the sick and infirm and even bringing the dead back to life—and the deep reverence his followers and the citizens had for him. The Archbishop told the Papal representative he would arrange for him to visit with Francis and check for himself what he had heard about this extraordinary holy man. The Archbishop designated one of his veteran priests, Father Carlo Perri, to accompany Monsignor Adorno. Father Perri was well known for his prudence and objectivity and had the complete trust of Francis and his friars.

Monsignor Adorno and Father Perri arrived at Paola in the early hours of the next morning and went immediately

to the monastery, entering the chapel. A priest was cele-
brating Mass, and, to one side, a friar was following the
Mass with deep concentration. The friar's great earnestness and fervid responses attracted the Papal envoy. He
had no doubt that this devout friar was the Saint he was
seeking. The prelate approached him, and kneeling,
reached out for Francis' hand to kiss it. But Francis,
startled, quickly withdrew his hand and said: "In the name
of Charity, Monsignor, it is I who should be kissing your
hand, consecrated for more than thirty years." At these
words, the Papal delegate was taken aback, wondering
how Francis could have had this background information
about him, when he knew that the Saint had had no
opportunity to know him and, as far as he knew, had not
been told of his coming. However, the monsignor realized
that his coming could not be unexpected because of the
Saint's well-known power of prophecy.

Francis invited Monsignor Adorno to his cell where, it
being winter, he hastened to have a brazier of coal brought
in. When the envoy had made himself as comfortable as
possible in the cramped, cold cell, the direct, straight-for-
ward cleric got down quickly to the purpose of his visit. He
said to Francis: "Brother Francis, I know of your manner
of living, and the way you want to perpetuate it through
your followers and your monasteries. I admire your forti-
tude. However, I must point out that this extreme form of
self-mortification is inconsistent with the demands of human nature, and is therefore condemned by the wisest men
of our age." The Saint listened attentively without the
slightest show of emotion. Monsignor Adorno continued:
"You cannot but agree with me, dear brother, that the observance of a strict fast for a lifetime, such as you insist on,
is an isolated phenomenon, capable of creating much admiration, but these requirements cannot be accepted as
part of an obligation for a religious order. It is therefore
necessary that you soften this excessively rigorous fasting
requirement if you are concerned with not exposing yourself and your followers to a way of living that will en-

danger your physical well-being. Because you are of sturdy peasant stock, you can withstand to a surprising extent this strict way of living, but it is not wise to impose it on those who may not be able to survive it."

Francis listened calmly to Monsignor Adorno's remarks. After a moment of silence, Francis arose, walked over to the brazier, and with both hands scooped up the burning embers. With the coals glowing like roses, he held them out to the startled monsignor, a matter-of-fact expression on his face. The Saint replied: "Yes, it is true Monsignor, I am only an unlearned peasant, and if I were not, I would not be able to do this." The monsignor, a man of much experience, did not miss the subtle irony in the statement.

Francis' action admitted no reply or any further objections from the prelate. The Saint had demonstrated through this incredible act that a man, sustained by the grace of God, can, without scorching himself, hold two handsful of live coals. Thus, through this same grace of God and personal commitment, such a man can live a healthy existence in the face of the most severe abstinence. The monsignor, overwhelmed by what he had just witnessed, dropped to his knees and tried to kiss the Saint's ash-blackened hands, but Francis withdrew them from him. Nevertheless, the monsignor reached for a fold of his well-worn tunic and kissed it.

Now completely convinced of the Saint's supernatural gifts and God-inspired wisdom, the monsignor, again the composed Papal representative, thought he would take advantage of the Saint's prophetic powers to determine how the civil strife that was raging in his home town, Genoa, would be finally resolved, particularly as it related to his noble family. The Saint told him that the fratricidal war would last some seventy years. (This is how it turned out.) It is said that Monsignor Adorno prepared a memorandum on the Saint's prophecy, which was passed on at his death to a nephew. However, the manuscript has been lost.

Satisfied with the results of his investigation, which were

far more impressive than what he had expected, Monsignor Adorno returned that same morning, with Father Perri, to the archbishop's chancery in San Lucido. He described to Archbishop Caracciolo the matters he had discussed with Francis and the Saint's scooping up of the red hot coals in his bare hands as an answer to his arguments. He assured the head of the Archdiocese of Paola that he was thoroughly convinced that Francis was all that he was said to be, a true saint and an authentic worker of miracles. With the archbishop's help, he interviewed many people from Paola and surrounding towns who were witnesses to the Saint's miraculous powers. Mainly they were individuals he had cured of long-standing diseases, cripples who had been made whole, blind people whose sight he had restored, deaf mutes who had regained the power of speech and hearing, including one of those who had died and had been brought back to life.

The Baron of Belmonte, Giacomo di Tarsia, appeared before the Papal envoy and reported on the Saint's miraculous cure of a long-standing running abscess in his leg, and the restoration to life of his dead son, Galeazzo. Francesco Rocco, the baby whose distorted features the Saint had realigned into a handsome face, also recounted this miracle worked by the Saint. Father Antonio Scozzetta related the incident when the Saint entered the roaring fire in a broken-down furnace at one of his monastery building sites and repaired it while in the midst of the fire. After taking many notes, Monsignor Adorno closed the hearing, satisfied that he had obtained more proof than he needed on the miraculous powers and extraordinary holiness of the Paolan Saint.

Paola's clergy, nobles, community leaders and people turned out in masses to accompany Monsignor Adorno to the outskirts of town, where they wished him God-speed on his journey back to Rome.

When the monsignor reached Rome, he made haste to arrange an audience with Pope Paul II to give an account of his visit to Calabria. Monsignor Adorno related the amazing cures that Francis had performed, the other things he had accomplished, his extraordinary piety and sincerity, his incredible divine powers, including the incident of the handsful of burning coals that he had personally witnessed. He told the Pope: "Holy Father, the fame of the Saint's extraordinary deeds, which has spread throughout Italy, and reached the ears of the Vicar of Christ, is in no way an exaggeration of the facts. Before my visit, I also was skeptical of what I had heard, but after seeing with my eyes and touching with my hands, I must repeat what the Queen of Sheba said about Soloman's wisdom, that I had not been told even half of the truth, and that the reality far exceeded anything that I had heard."

Monsignor Adorno's report on the Saint gladdened the Pope's heart, who, despite the worldly pomp and circumstance that surrounded him, was trying to restore the spirit of Christianity in the world. There is reason to believe that the Pope wrote to Archbishop Caracciolo, asking him to be most considerate of the Saint, his followers and his mission. However, because Paul II believed the fast was too dangerous for the physical well-being of the monks, he refused to give the Order Papal sanction. Despite the Pope's public attitude, Francis issued a written order to his followers that in addition to the vows of eternal obedience, chastity, and poverty, the hermit friars must continue to abstain from meat, eggs, milk, and similar animal derivatives.

On July 26, 1471, a few months after Monsignor Adorno's return from his visit to Francis, Pope Paul II, who had always been a robust man, died during the night from an apoplectic stroke. Some see the hand of God in his untimely death. On August 9, Francesco della Rovere, from Savona, on the Genoese coast, succeeded to the Papal throne as Sixtus IV. He had been superior general of Franciscan Conventuals Minor. He was a pious and holy man with deep scholarly knowledge of theological matters, and his election was widely hailed in Calabria, where it was felt that, as a Franciscan monk, he would have a clearer understanding of fasting, abstinence, and self-mortification, such as practiced by the Minimi.

Chapter 8

THE POPE APPROVES

Early in 1471, with a growing number of monasteries and followers, the Saint became aware of the need for writing down certain simple rules which his hermit friars must follow to achieve the self-mortification and sanctity essential for achieving the supernatural goal that God had entrusted to him and his disciples.

Before beginning to write the rules, he first asked for the approval of Archbishop Pirro Caracciolo of Cosenza. The archbishop, a long-time champion of Francis, quickly approved the request. Francis then enlisted the help of his confessor and one of his earliest disciples, Father Baldassare Spino, a learned man and, like himself, a native of Paola. The first rules were those of all penitential monastic orders, vows of perpetual poverty, chastity, and obedience—essential to any religious life. Furthermore, as an additional penance, he required the acceptance of perpetual fasting and complete abstinence from meat, eggs, milk, and all other animal food stuffs, except in case of illness—when a physician might prescribe a change in diet for the duration of the condition under treatment. The dress was to be the established simple brown tunic, a hood to be pulled over the head during inclement weather, and simple, open-toe sandals, though the preference, whenever possible, was for bare feet.

Also established were the number of hours for prayer and the various prayers to be recited each day and night. The final rule was a comprehensive one requiring the hermit monks at all times and under all conditions to be ready, singly or with other friars, to fulfill the spiritual and temporal needs of people of all stations that they would encounter in their daily rounds. The eternal motto to be kept in mind was *"Caritas"*—Charity—to one and all.

During the period in which the Hermit Friars were founded—a time of deep self-indulgence, cynical selfishness, and arrogance—these were incredibly strict rules, as Pope Paul II had indicated. Yet constantly new followers joined the Order and cheerfully vowed to observe these rules and to follow the Saint's example. Many of the disciples were members of the nobility, accustomed to luxury and rich living. There were few instances of friars, once accepted, returning to the outside world. Strangely enough, no copies of these first rules, apparently distributed to then existing monasteries, have survived. However, they were all incorporated into the more formal rules prepared in France in 1483, twelve years later.

According to Father Giovanni da Milazzo, the coat of arms that the Saint designed for the Order—a shield with the word *"CARITAS"* in gold letters on a light blue field, topped by a crown, proof of the divine nobility of the organization—came to him while in ecstatic prayer in his cell, probably in Milazzo. While in this deep, religious communion, an angel appeared to him with the shield shining brightly on his arm. The angel, holding out the shield, said: "Francis, this shall be the shield of your order." After this incident, Francis became even further removed from worldly concern, living not only on charity but for charity. Charity to all was to be the major goal and distinction of his mission. It was this single-minded commitment to universal charity that made him and his followers so deeply respected and popular among people in all walks of life. He insisted that his hermit friars mingle constantly among the people, rendering them whatever service was needed, particularly spritual help. Francis himself set an example. Every day, he moved conspicuously through the crowds, exchanging greetings and dispensing his blessing, and, of course, curing the sick and consoling the downcast and the unfortunates. During the difficult times that prevailed in those days and the cruel

and tyrannical rule of the feudal lords and their under-
lings, the presence of the penitent brothers was a great
blessing to the peasants and the poor, so sadly neglected
by the government.

The angel who appeared to Francis in the vision was St.
Michael, one of the archangels. At the request of the Saint,
this archangel was made the Protector of the Order, which
at that time was named "The Congregation of the Hermit
Friars of Brother Francis of Paola." Archbishop Caracciolo of Consenza, who had been from the beginning Francis' warmest supporter, officially sanctioned this title on
November 30, 1471. The archbishop, in his letter of approval, also made it clear that he unreservedly approved
what Francis had done and was doing and would be glad to
help in any way possible to further his plans and ambitions. He also approved the rules that Francis and Father
Spino had drawn up, and gave Francis and the superiors of
the various monasteries authority to prevail upon any
priest (member of an order, or secular) to celebrate a Mass
at dawn for the monks, when none of their own priests was
available.

Archbishop Caracciolo authorized the clerical members of the Order to perform all priestly duties, such as
hearing confessions, dispensing Communion, marrying,
and conferring the Last Rites, and granted that the monks
could acquire whatever land they needed in the archdiocese to erect new monasteries and churches. In short, they
were to have all the rights and privileges enjoyed by the
Franciscans and other cloistered orders. And finally, he
stated that Francis' congregation would be ecclesiastically
outside the jurisdiction of the archbishop and all his successors, subject forever directly to the Supreme Pontiff.
The archbishop's sweeping concessions, which may have
been of doubtful validity as they related to his successors,
were obviously a move to influence the Holy See to give
Francis' congregation full recognition and approval so
that the monks could establish their monasteries anywhere
in the world. The archbishop's strategy bore fruit almost

immediately.

With the untimely demise of Paul II (1471), Francis sensed a radical change at the Vatican. Paul, though sympathetic to the Saint's miraculous achievements and divine powers (confirmed for him as factual by his delegate, Monsignor Adorno), had adamantly refused to approve what he considered a too strict dietary requirement. The new Pope, Francesco Cardinal della Rovere, a Genoese Franciscan, had a better understanding of and appreciation for fasting and self-mortification for religious dedicated to meditation and to the service of unfortunates. Francis decided, therefore, to take positive steps to obtain full official Vatican recognition of his congregation of hermit friars.

Toward the end of 1471, he dispatched to Rome his most trusted and scholarly follower, Father Spino, so that, as an emissary of the great Miracle Worker, he could personally submit the seal of approval given him by the archbishop of Cosenza. Father Spino, who had also obtained a special letter of introduction from the archbishop, had no difficulty in getting a private audience with Pope Sixtus IV (1471-1484), who was more than favorably disposed to Francis' request. The Pope indicated that he would have to submit the petition to the College of Cardinals before making a final decision, but he anticipated no problems. In the meantime, Fr. Spino assumed the position of procurator-general for the Order at the Vatican, and continued in that office until Francis called him to Tours, France, in 1493.

In Rome, Father Spino established a recovery for the Hermit Friars in an unpretentious house near the Church of St. Anastasia, where the monks could practice their religious life. The new mission was quickly filled with recruits from the Roman area, and the friars were soon conspicuous in the poorer sections of the Eternal City, going about fulfilling their chores of charity and consolation to the deprived.

The Pope, wishing to follow long-established, standard

ecclesiastical procedures, requested the reactions of his cardinals to the investigations made in Calabria by his predecessor, Pius II, through Monsignor Adorno. Also, on June 19, 1473, he wrote to the Bishop of San Marco Argentaro, a town which, though located in the Archdiocese of Cosenza, was directly under the Holy See in Rome. The presiding bishop was Goffredo di Castro, of Tropea, who had been bishop of Martirano before being transferred in 1446. The Pope sought further information from Archbishop Caracciolo on matters included in his special letter transmitted through Fr. Spino. But more, Sixtus IV wanted to be certain that there would be no objections or conflict in the Church in granting the necessary concessions to the Hermit Friars. He received a glowing report from Bishop Goffredo, indicating that, according to the Archbishop of Cosenza, such official recognition would be in the highest interest of the Church and of the Christian world, and that there could be nothing but exemplary Christian charity and piety to be expected from Francis' hermits—with which the College of Cardinals subsequently agreed. The Pope, therefore, gave blanket approval to the congregation, including all ecclesiastical privileges, indulgences, and rights enjoyed by all the other special orders of the Church. As soon as the Vatican decision reached Archbishop Caracciolo in Cosenza, he immediately caused the constitution for the Order to be printed and distributed under the title "Constitution of the Congregation of the Hermit Friars of Brother Francis of Paola."

The King of Naples, then Ferdinand of Aragon, known as "Ferrante" ("the Iron-like"), on being advised of the Pope's approval of the congregation, sent Francis an official letter placing the monastery and church in Paola, the first built, under his special protection and granting the Hermit Friars there special favors. The royal document, which was dated April 23, 1473, written in Latin, still exists in the Minimi archives.

However, Francis was not quite satisfied with the ap-

proval notice issued by the Pope. He wanted blanket authority from the Vatican to permit the establishment of his
monasteries in any archdiocese or diocese in the Christian
world, completely beyond the control of the local bishops
or archbishops or any authority except the Pope himself.
On May 17, 1474, Sixtus IV issued such a decree, placing
the Order under the direct supervision of the Popes. The
constitution of the congregation was reprinted under the
official sanction of the Holy See. With this universal approval by the Pope, canonically recognizing the congregation as co-equal with all other mendicant orders, Francis
was free to carry on his mission anywhere within the
sphere of the Church. The Pope's action made Francis extremely pleased and he thanked God for having obtained
this great favor.

However, Francis' happiness did not last long. He was
greatly disturbed when he was informed that Sixtus IV had
officially established him as superior general of his congregation, in perpetuity. He felt that the title was too ex-
alted and out of keeping with the humility and unpretentious life he lived. He wrote to the Pope, pointing out that
he did not want such a title, furthermore that he was not
ordained, and that Fr. Spino, an ordained priest and emi-
nent theologian, would be the more proper person to as-
sume such a title. But the Pope, even more impressed by
the Saint's protest and humble attitude, and fully cogni-
zant of Francis' leadership and organizational ability, refused to reconsider and told him that all such protests
would be useless. The Saint, though disappointed, resigned
himself to the Pope's decision, accepting it as the will of
God.

Though he quickly established himself as a model superior general, acting with exemplary firmness and wisdom in governing the newly recognized congregation, and
in promoting and expanding it, he continued to live as
humbly as he had before, in meditation, prayer, and service to the poor, and in carrying out the most menial tasks
of the community. He was fifty-six years of age when the

Pope declared him superior general of his order, an office he held for thirty-six years.

Chapter 9

FRANCIS AS PROPHET

The Saint's gift of prophecy was second only to his power to perform miracles, and he was fully aware that both were gifts from God, over which he had only nominal control. In certain instances, he knew clearly what was going to happen regardless of what he might do, and then his power to perform miracles was unavailing. He was helpless before the will of God and His plans.

One famous instance concerned the husband of the Princess Polissena, wife of Henry of Aragon, the son of King Ferdinand I of Naples. She was a great admirer and patron of the Saint and thoroughly convinced of his miraculous powers. However, she was to learn the Saint's powers were limited. The royal pair were in Gerace when her husband, Prince Henry, became gravely ill. Deeply concerned, the princess sent a servant to the Paterno monastery where the Saint was staying, begging him to intervene with God to cure her husband. Francis, through his power of prophecy, knew instantly that the prince was doomed—completely beyond his power to save him. He told the servant sadly: "The sickness of your prince is not curable, because God wants him with Him. In a few days he will be no more." However, to soften the blow, Francis sat down and wrote a letter to the devoted princess, recommending certain meaningless remedies, fully aware that they would be useless. Three days later the prince passed away as the Saint had predicted.

On another occasion, Bellino del Fiore, who had been miraculously cured from a grave illness by the Saint, was on his way to the monastery with his very sick son in his arms when he met Francis on the road. Bellino, grief-stricken, asked the Saint to save his son. The Saint shook his head, and said with deep sorrow: "This child is the tenth that the Lord wants from you!" Shortly thereafter the child died.

Perhaps his most amazing prophecy was one that involved him personally. During the building of the monastery at Paola, Francis was at the bottom of a hill, helping prepare material for the building, when a cart, used to transport building material, slid off an upper road and came crashing down on him, breaking some ribs and dislocating his leg. In great alarm the workers rushed to help him. They found him unconscious. They carried him into the monastery and laid him down tenderly on the floor. Regaining consciousness, Francis told them: "In the name of Charity, brothers, let me lay here on the floor and return to your work. The good Lord wants that Brother Body should rest here for forty days. Do not worry, for then I will be well again!" However, he did permit them to place him on two boards, where he remained without other care for the forty days he had prophesied. On the last day, the boards began to move around so that it was not possible for the Saint to remain on them. So he arose, and to the wonderment of everyone, walked around in perfect health.

A curious example of this mysterious prophetic power was the one in which a peasant from Belmonte named Giacomo Ronco, whose son, on whom he doted, was suffering from an illness that had left him near death. He decided to ask Francis to cure him. He brought the Saint a basket of cherries from his orchard. The basket was only half full, so he went into the cherry orchard of his uncle, which was next to his, and proceeded to fill the basket. When Giacomo presented the basket to the Saint, the Saint said nothing but began to sort out the cherries of Giacomo's orchard from those of his uncle's orchard. After he had completed this task, he said: "Dear brother, I accept the fruit that is from your orchard, but I cannot accept that which belongs to another." Giacomo was greatly confused and did not know what to expect, but the Saint soon reassured him and told him: "The sickness that has struck down your son is not fatal. In a few days he will be completely cured. However, in the future be sure that you respect the belongings of others so that you can enjoy always the grace of God." Francesco Rogato, a witness at the Cosentine canonization hearings in 1512 told of a similar case when Francis refused to accept a basket of figs from an admirer because he knew that they had not come from his garden, much to the embarrassment of the poor peasant.

Matteo Cappellano, of Rossano, had living with him a deaf relative who was bedridden. He became quite concerned when another relative, also living with him, became seriously ill as well. Unable to handle the situation, Matteo decided to call on the great Miracle Worker of Paola in the hope that he would help his two unfortunate relatives. When Francis had heard Matteo's plea, he told him: "My dear brother, your deaf relative will soon leave her bed, completely recovered, because of her lively faith in God; but the other one will soon appear before the Divine Presence because she has had so little faith and so little concern for salvation during her life." Matteo returned home to his ailing relatives, quite disturbed by what the Saint had prophesied. Soon, events occurred as Francis had predicted.

Another case of Francis' ability to read the future involved a young wife, whose name has not been recorded, who had been ailing for a long time. After trying many remedies, she decided to approach the famous Miracle Worker in the hope that he could restore her to perfect health. Francis immediately realized that the young lady's problem stemmed primarily from the state of her soul, rather than her body. He listened patiently to her problems and then said: "Take care, in the name of Charity, to learn to live as a good Christian, for the remaining days of your life are few." The Saint's admonition put the poor woman into shock. With all hope of regaining her health gone, she became terribly depressed and apathetic. In hope of being able to raise her out of her despair, her husband went to Francis to ask his advice. Francis told him "Your wife has been conceded seven more years of life by God. Tell her to prepare herself for death, which cannot frighten those who lead a good life." The woman, when told by her husband what the Saint had said, snapped out of her depression, altered her way of living, and took measures to improve her spiritual well-being. As Francis had predicted, she died seven years later, a worthy Christian.

A famous historical prediction relates to the fratricidal wars between the Italian city-states that were devastating the Peninsula and causing great suffering among people of all classes. The de Medici family, which had become tremendously wealthy through commerce, had ruled Florence since 1250. The de Medicis' most bitter rivals were the banking family of the Pazzis. On April 26, 1478, the Pazzis, in an attempt to wrest the rule of Florence from Lorenzo de Medici, attacked Lorenzo and his brother, Giuliano, while they were attending Mass in the Cathedral of Florence. Giuliano was stabbed to death, but Lorenzo escaped through the sacristy. Because the nephews of Pope Sixtus IV and Archbishop Salviati of Florence were allied with the Pazzis, Lorenzo, later known as "The Magnificent," accused the Pope of helping the conspirators. Sixtus IV excommunicated Lorenzo, put Florence under Papal interdiction, and with the help of King Ferrante of Naples, made war against the Medicis. This is known in history as the *Guerra Toscana* or the Tuscan War. Several Tuscan city-states had taken sides (Siena siding with the Pope). Gian Galeazzo Sforza, the Duke of Milan and husband of Isabella, the daughter of King Ferrante of Naples, sided with Florence against the Pope and his father-in-law.

This internecine war resulted in heavy taxation and the drafting of young men for the Neopolitan army. This was of concern to all Calabrians. Francesco Florio, a close follower of Francis, decided to find out what would be the final result of this terrible war. He asked the Saint: "Father, you who are possessed with the spirit of God, what will happen in this terrible war in Tuscany?" Francis, without hesitation, told him: "Have no fears; before you know it, the belligerents will come to an understanding." The prophecy came true when Lorenzo and the King of Naples came to terms.

Though Lorenzo scornfully refused the peace offering which Sixtus IV made in April 1479, several months later, as matters became worse for him and his allies, the Pope sought out Ferrante, the King of Naples. Ferrante, a man of weak loyalty, agreed to conditions that were not in accordance with those the Pope had proposed, but the Pope was forced to accept them in order to unite the Italian states against the threatening invasion of Italy by the Turks.

Some other examples of the Saint's ability accurately to predict future happenings are the following:

Andrea di Rosetto, a shoemaker of Paola, was very attached to the Saint and enjoyed his close friendship. One day, in the autumn of 1478, Francis said to him: "My dear Andrea, do not fail to buy as quickly as possible all of this year's grain that you can store so that it will be available throughout next year." "But grain is so plentiful that it costs almost nothing," Andrea replied. "You do what I tell you, and you will have no reason to regret it," Francis told him. The shoemaker hastened to do as the Saint had suggested. The next year the harvest was extremely poor, and the price of grain went sky high. Needless to say, the shoemaker and his family were most grateful to the Saint for his prophetic warning.

Another resident of Paola, a farmer called Calvano de Plantedi, was out tilling his fields one day when the Saint passed by on his way to obtain lumber for a new building. The farmer came over to pay his respects to the great Miracle Worker. The Saint restrained him as Calvano started to return to his work and warned him: "In the name of Charity, this year do not only sow your fields, but also take special care of your vineyards." Calvano went back to his fields, puzzled by what he had been told, but determined to follow out the Saint's instructions, though he knew that the harvest for 1478 was going to be an exceptional one. In 1479, all of Calabria, and presumably most of Southern Italy, suffered a great drought. The Saint's prophetic warning was reported by Calvano himself at the canonization hearings at Cosenza in 1512.

Francis' reputation as a prophet plus as a worker of great miracles spread throughout Italy and reached the Vatican and the various royal courts. It made the great and the famous of the day interested in meeting this extraordinary man.

Chapter 10

THE TURKISH THREAT

While the Italian states and cities were fighting among themselves—for and against the Pope—the Ottoman Turks were conquering Eastern Europe. In 1416 the Venetians temporarily stopped the advance of the all-conquering Turks when Doge Loredano's fleet scored a major victory in the Dardanelles and forced the reigning sultan to sue for peace. The Venetians also took over the control of Salonika and made an alliance with the Greek Emperor against the Turks.

But in 1425 the Turkish fleet forced the Venetians out of their Aegean ports and captured Salonika. The Venetians, preoccupied with fighting the Milanese—from whom they wrested the cities of Verona, Vicenza, Brescia, Bergamo, and Cremona—had to bow to Turkish demands. Thus did civil wars between Italian states help the Turkish infidels achieve the conquest of the Balkan nations.

In 1453 the Venetians helped the Greek Emperor and other Balkan leaders defend Constantinople from the Turks, led by Sultan Mohammed II. With the fall of Constantinople, the Turks overran Greece, Albania, Serbia and the eastern coast of the Adriatic. In 1470 the Venetians lost the ports of Negropont (Chalcis) on Euboea, an island off Athens; Lemnos Island, off the mouth of the Dardanelles; and Scutari in northern Albania. Thereafter the Venetians had to pay tribute to the Turks to continue trade in the Aegean Sea area. Venice, however, retained control of Cyprus (which is today in dispute between the Greeks and the modern Turks). The Treaty of Constantinople in 1479 gave the Turks complete control of the Adriatic, Ionian, and Aegean Seas and removed the Venetian fleet as a bulwark against attack on the Italian Peninsula.

The continuing conquests of the Ottoman Turks did not escape the attention of the Saint, in spite of his many preoccupations. He was fully aware of the danger to the Catholic Church and to his native land and blamed the various Italian leaders, especially King Ferdinand of Naples, who was wasting money, manpower and materials in the futile wars in the Tuscan area. Francis was wondering whether King Ferrante could be forced to realize the threat to his kingdom as a result of Turkish victories over Venice and her Balkan allies. In his trips around Paterno, only too aware of the great storm that would soon strike Italy, he begged all those he encountered—friars, workers, neighbors, and visitors from other areas—to pray, do penance and ask God's intercession against the advancing foe of Christianity.

Father Giacomo Guerrieri, from the Cathedral at Nicastro, on the northwest coast of the province of Cantanzaro, visited the Saint at Paterno. After the visit, Francis gave him three apples, one for himself, the other for the Princess Polissena who resided in Gerace, on the southern coast of Calabria in the province of Cantanzaro and whose husband he was not able to save from dying, and the third to the Bishop of Nicastro. "Tell the Monsignor [the Bishop] that at every morning Mass he must recite the collect against the Turks, because never, as today, is there such a threat to our religion and our country." According to Father Guerrieri, at that time no one was aware of the Turkish threat to the Christians in Italy and Western Europe.

At the time of Father Guerrieri's visit, the King of Naples was still concentrating his military forces in the struggle between the Pope and Florence in Tuscany. Francesco Florio, who earlier had asked him to prophesy the outcome of the war in Tuscany, again queried the Saint. He replied with some anxiety: "It is not with Tuscany, but with our own kingdom that we must be concerned. I see the Turks soon invading our land! Let us try to placate with good works and prayers the Most High, whom we have angered with our iniquities."

The Saint set an example for those who followed him by further mortifying himself, fasting more strictly, and praying more fervently. In his prayers he even offered himself as a possible victim to be sacrificed for the good of his country. Evidently God had other plans for him.

Wherever he appeared publicly, he was always despondent, exhorting his listeners to pray fervently to God and the saints in Heaven to spare their land from this terrible punishment for the ungodliness that prevailed in Christian countries. The Saint's persistent public appeals for prayers and penance against the Turks were reported at the Cosentine canonization hearings of 1512 by Luigi Paladino, the royal auditor of Cosenza, and Calvano di Plantedi, already mentioned.

According to Antonio Giordano and several other canonization witnesses, three months before the capture of Otranto, then a flourishing port at the end of the heel of the Italian boot on the Adriatic Sea, the Saint predicted the exact date on which Otranto would fall—the 28th day of July 1480. He always ended these appeals by urging his listeners to fast and do penance to appease the wrath of God. Concerning Otranto, it is said that on one occasion Francis rose in the presence of all his friars, bowed his head and in a voice full of anguish, cried out: "Unhappy city! How many corpses do I see strewn in your streets! By how much Christian blood will they be flooded!"

But the Hermit Saint did not limit his prophetic concern to pleas for prayers and penance from the people. He decided to take direct action. He wrote a letter to the King of Naples, begging him to stop involving himself in Italian civil wars and to turn his attention to fortifying his cities on the Adriatic and Ionian Seas so they could resist the coming Turkish invasion. Ferrante ignored the Saint's urgent appeal and on the advice of his ministers continued to meddle in Italian quarrels. Undaunted by the King's arrogant rebuff, Francis sent him a second and more urgent letter through a Neapolitan captain, who had come to see him at Paterno before taking his ship to Rome. In this letter he begged Ferrante to take steps to protect his eastern cities from the bloody incursions of the Turks. Ferrante ignored this second plea also, dismissing the Turks as no particular threat to Italy or to his kingdom and the Saint as a religious fanatic suffering from delusions. In fact, Francis' letters, with their implications that Ferrante was neglecting his subjects and his duty, angered the egotistical monarch. He bitterly resented the Saint's interference, and this resentment later turned into persecution, though the Saint's warning about the Turkish threat soon became a reality.

On July 28, 1480, a fleet of Turkish ships, numbering ninety galleys and 18,000 soldiers, under the command of Achmet Pasha, came out of Valona in Albania and attacked Otranto, one of the busiest ports on the Adriatic side of Italy. The Pasha's demands for surrender of the city were rejected by the ill-armed but determined Otrantons. The Turks laid siege to the port, subjecting it to continuous bombardment and daily assaults, all courageously repulsed by the poorly armed and poorly trained citizens, fighting gallantly in hope of help from King Ferrante. However, on the 11th of August, the Turks crushed all resistance and poured into the city, burning, looting, and massacring the defenders. The Archbishop, Stefano Pendinelli, was in his Cathedral just finishing Mass, with hundreds of frightened old people, women and children crowded together, when the Turks burst down the doors and slaughtered all those in the church. They then tortured the archbishop and his priests before killing them.

The next day Achmet ordered that all the surviving men over the age of fifteen be rounded up in his presence. More than 800 were found. He told them that if they would embrace the religion of Mohammed and deny that of Christ, he would free them with their wives and children and let them live in peace. Antonio Primaldo, acting as their spokesman, told the Pasha defiantly that they preferred to die rather than to deny their religion and their conscience. His companions shouted in unison that he spoke for them all. On August 14, Achmet ordered the 800 brought before his tent, which had been pitched on Minerva Hill, just outside the city. He then ordered that the prisoners' heads be chopped off, starting with their leader, Primaldo. He watched the execution with admiration for the courage of these brave men so sadly neglected by their king. Since the slaughter of these men, Minerva Hill has been called the Mount of the Martyrs, and the victims were declared blessed in 1771 by Pope Clement XIV.

Fourteen months later, October 13, 1481, Prince Alfonso, Duke of Calabria, Ferrante's son, recaptured the devastated city and, as a belated act of honor, arranged to have the bodies of the 800 martyrs buried in the cathedral. Later, in 1540, the people of Otranto, who had been advised of Francis' repeated attempts to have the King of Naples fortify their city against a Turkish attack, arranged to have a Minimi monastery built on the Mount of the Martyrs as a reward for his futile efforts.

The capture and destruction of Otranto by the Turks alarmed all the Italian states. Most alarmed was Ferrante himself, vividly recalling the warnings of the Saint from Paola. He hastened to recall his son Alfonso, commanding the Neapolitan troops in Tuscany and ordered him to move against the Turks. In the meantime, he called on the Pope and the Italian princes to come to his assistance. Only the Pope responded, even though he had been betrayed by the treacherous Ferrante when he tried to arrange a just peace among the warring Italian factions. Sixtus sent appeals not only to all Italian princes but to all the reigning heads of Europe to unite against the Turks. He requested that all money and military aid possible be sent to King Ferrante. He also ordered that one-tenth of all money collected by the churches be turned over to the Neapolitan monarch and granted indulgences remitting the punishment due to sins of Christians who, in the name of Christ, joined in the war against the invaders.

With this help King Ferrante was able to mobilize a powerful army, under the command of the Duke of Calabria, and a fleet of ships, under the celebrated captain Villamarino. Ferrante's positive reaction was hailed by the Saint, who, in addition to his special prayers and penance on behalf of the enterprise, continued his exhortations to the people to persist in their pleas to God to thwart the enemies of Christ.

One of the Duke of Calabria's most trusted captains, Gian Nicola Conclubet, the Count of Arena, and one of Francis' most devoted followers, marched his troops through Paterno and stopped for the Saint's blessing. Francis knew the count to be not only a brave and competent soldier but also a most pious man, and was overjoyed to see him. He gave him and his troops his blessing and promised to pray for their success; plus, he gave each soldier a small candle he had blessed, saying: "Dear Count, go without fear and with the grace of God; you will fight with great valor against the enemies of our Faith; victory will be yours, and you and your soldiers shall return safely to your homes." One of the soldiers refused to accept the candle, saying that he did not believe in religious articles. All the other soldiers accepted the offering with humility. It is reported that all the soldiers returned home safely except the one who had rejected the candle.

During a battle, one of the count's officers was struck by a cannon ball, which broke his arm. The surgeons believed that it would be necessary to amputate it. Father Giovanni Genovese, who had been designated by Francis as chaplain for the troops, visited the wounded man. He asked him to unwrap his arm; then he made the Sign of the Cross over it, and instantaneously it became whole again.

During the height of the fighting at Otranto, Nicola Castelli of Paola came to the Saint, seeking divine protection on behalf of his brother-in-law, Nicola Picardi, one of the captains of King Ferrante's mounted guards and a man of great courage and skill. No sooner had Nicola explained to Francis the reason for his call than the Saint told him with great sorrow: "Brother, resign yourself; our dear friend Nicola is no more; he has died a martyr!"

Captain Picardi's daring and leadership had attracted the attention of the Turkish commander-in-chief. He ordered his soldiers to take steps to make him prisoner. In front of a fortified area on the outskirts of Otranto where Picardi was stationed, the Turks dug a deep hole and then covered it over with branches. In the morning they massed on top of the fortified point, daring Picardi to attack them. Picardi, at the head of his men, led a charge over the trap and plunged into the hole. His men, bewildered by the loss of their captain, retreated and the Turks took Picardi prisoner. They brought him to Achmet, who lauded his courage and leadership and offered him a high command in his army if he would become a Mohammedan. The Calabrian captain indignantly spurned the Pasha's offer, though Achmet pleaded with him. Realizing finally that Picardi would rather die than betray his religion and country, he ordered his execution.

In April of 1481, while the Italian allies were laying siege to Otranto, Francis shut himself in his cell for eight days in fervent prayer and meditation. At the end of the eighth day he came out smiling and happy, announcing to his friars: "Blessed be God, brothers, He has decided to take pity on us! Shortly the Turks will be cast out of our land."

Soon word reached the embattled troops that Sultan Mohammed II, the Turks' great military leader, had died suddenly from an attack of colic on May 3, 1481. He was only 53 years of age and had been in perfect health. His oldest son, Bajazet II, succeeded to the Sultanate, but his second son, Zizim, opposed him, and a civil war broke out among the Turks, forcing them to abandon further plans to invade Italy and Western Europe. On September 8, the Turks surrendered Otranto and thus ended for a time their threat to Europe and the Christian world. It is interesting to note that when he died, Mohammed II had recruited an army of 300,000 men with the apparent intention of over-running Europe and converting it to Mohammedism. While locked for eight days in his cell, St. Francis of Paola, through his fervent pleas to God, may have saved Western Civilization. This could have been his greatest miracle!

Chapter II

FRANCIS AND THE KING OF NAPLES

With the Turkish menace removed, through his earnest and fervent prayers for mercy from an angry God, Francis turned his attention to his ever increasing number of monasteries and followers. Unfortunately, some of the courtiers at the court of King Ferrante in Naples, jealous of the growing popularity of the Miracle Worker of Paola, and looking for a scapegoat to curry the unscrupulous King's favor, decided to plot together to denounce Francis as a pious troublemaker who was stirring up the Calabrians against the King.

They pointed out to the fickle despot that Francis, in his travels around the Calabrian region, sympathized with the people's complaints about the heavy taxes and the cruel methods used by the King's tax collectors to collect them. Also, the courtiers reminded Ferrante that the Saint, two years before, had repeatedly called on the King to stop meddling in the squabbles between the Italian states, and to concentrate his energies on preparing the Neapolitan armies to repulse the coming invasion of the Turks. Nothing daunting him, moreover, Francis on his own part continued publicly to admonish Ferrante, his children, and ministers to amend their brutal attitudes, to cease flagrant abuses against the people, and to establish a competent and humane administration.

Needless to say, the cynical courtiers were pleased to hear of the Hermit Saint's continuous denunciations and arranged that news of the Saint's public protests should reach the King's ears in their most inflammatory and alarming form.

Since 1477, the good people of Castellamare di Stabia, a few miles south of Naples, had been begging the Saint of Paola to come to their town and establish a monastery for Hermit Friars. They offered Francis a small church, called Saint Mary of Pozzano, and promised sufficient money so that a monastery could be built beside it. After careful thought, the Saint decided to take advantage of the offer and, having obtained the approval of Archbishop Alessio Certa, head of the archdiocese of Naples, sent two of his veteran friars to arrange to build the monastery.

When this news reached the court, the courtiers who despised Francis rushed to Ferrante saying: "The measure is full. The pious rebel is pitching tent within the capital. Any hesitation now in denouncing and punishing him would be most dangerous. It will give this false prophet an opportunity to incite the people to revolt."

The suspicious Ferrante could not resist the implications. With a show of righteous indignation, he ordered that the Hermit Friars be expelled from the monastery of Pozzano, in Calabria. He sent a band of fifty soldiers to Calabria, under one of his most trusted captains, to bring Francis back to Naples, bound as a prisoner. The troops left immediately for Pozzano.

While the soldiers were on their way to capture Francis and destroy his monastery, Cardinal Giovanni d'Aragona, second son of Ferrante, proceeded to evict the Hermit Friars from the new monastery at Castellamare. This prince, arrogant as his father, refused to listen to reason or prayers, and flatly refused all requests from the friars for time to make other arrangements. What especially frightened the humble friars was the fact that, as a cardinal of the Church, he should have protected them from such arbitrary action. The evicted monks hurried to Pozzano to apprise their founder of what had happened. The Saint showed no alarm or great concern, counseling his disturbed disciples to accept the Cardinal's action as the Will of God, Who directs all things in the best interest of everyone.

Cardinal Giovanni ordered the complete demolition of the Castellamare monastery and, to make sure that the Hermit Friars would never regain control of the site, rebuilt it into a villa for his own use. However, Giovanni, who, because of his royal parentage had been consecrated a cardinal by Sixtus IV in 1477 (when only 18 years of age) did not long enjoy the fruit of his arrogance and hypocrisy. Giovanni died in Rome at age twenty-five.

By the time the captain and his soldiers reached Cosenza, the content of Ferrante's order against Francis and his monasteries had spread throughout Calabria. The citizens were deeply shocked, and their leaders confronted the captain of the troops in an attempt to persuade him that the order was obviously due to a misunderstanding or to the action of those who hated Francis and that he should not carry it out. However, the captain pointed out that he had no choice in the matter; whether right or wrong, he had to do what the King ordered. Through hostile groups of watchers that lined each side of the road, the troops marched to Paterno, where the Saint was located at the time. The watchers, through their silence, made clear their resentment.

The Saint, who was being kept informed of developments, showed no particular concern, retiring quietly to his cell for prayer and meditation. From many sources he had been offered help to flee, but he flatly refused to take advantage of these offers, saying that he had no reason to fear what was to happen. His own monks, thrown into consternation by his refusal to take steps to protect himself, begged him to arrange it so that he would not be readily found. He rebuffed them saying: "My dear brothers, we are in the house of God, and I am sure that He will know how to protect us. If God wills that I should be taken prisoner, let us bow with proper humility to the Almighty's holy will. But if that is not His will, then there is no force on earth that could harm one hair of my head." So saying, he went into the church, knelt before the high altar where the Holy Eucharist was kept, and immersed himself deeply in prayer.

When the soldiers arrived at the Paterno monastery, they methodically searched all the cells and other sections of the church and monastery compound, crossing and recrossing the place in the church where the Saint was praying. However, they could not see him. As it had happened on other occasions, Francis had become invisible to his enemies. The soldiers, baffled and angry, searched the premises again and again, unable to understand why they could not find him, though they were assured that he had not left the monastery grounds and that he was not in hiding or doing anything else to avoid them.

The soldiers, thoroughly aroused, began to curse and threaten the friars and the workers with physical violence if they did not reveal the whereabouts of the Saint. A worker, who had been following the soldiers' futile hunt and now fearing possible injury over their frustrations, said to the captain: "How is it possible that you do not see the Servant of God when you and your men have passed by him many times?" "That is not possible," shouted the captain angrily. "Where is he then?" The worker led him into the church and pointed out the Saint kneeling deep in prayer in front of the high altar. The captain, suddenly aware of the holy powers of the Saint, dropped to his knees before him, begging his forgiveness. "In the name of Charity," the Saint told him, "get up from your knees and do not fear. You are merely the executor of someone else's orders. Return to the King, and tell him for me, that he is a person of little faith to believe that my presence before him would in some way be useful to him. Tell him that it is best for him to amend his personal behavior and to reform his government, or else he and his household shall not be able to avoid the punishment of divine justice."

After this admonition, the Saint indicated that he had forgiven all that had occurred and gave the captain several devotional tokens (rosaries and holy candles that he had blessed) to take to the King and Queen and their children. He then invited the captain and his soldiers to the refectory where he found two loaves of bread and a jug of wine.

He blessed and distributed the bread and wine among them, and all found both to be delicious and plentiful. In fact, there was bread and wine left over after all had eaten their fill. The fifty soldiers and the captain were stunned by this incredible miracle, so similar to miracles that Christ had performed during His ministry. Overwhelmed with remorse over their treatment of the Saint and his friars before they witnessed the Saint's divine powers, the repentant captain and soldiers knelt down and again asked the Saint for his forgiveness. The Saint prayed the captain to deliver the religious items he had given him to the royal family. Then he blessed them all and told them to return to Naples, confident in the grace of God.

The captain realized that when he returned to the court he would be in a most difficult position to explain what had occurred. He was returning not only without the Saint the King had ordered him to capture, but with a message that could only infuriate Ferrante. However, he felt that the Saint's miraculous powers would permit him to deliver Francis' blunt message so that the King would accept it with proper grace. He knew that Francis and his friars were praying for the successful completion of a unique mission and a radical and miraculous change in the King's attitude. The King, strangely subdued, listened as the captain recited the events that had occurred: The incredible search for the Saint, who all the time was in plain view before the high altar but invisible to them; the Saint's humility and generosity; the miracle of the bread and wine; and the deep affection in which the Calabrian people held him. Even the courtiers who hated Francis listened with wonderment. The King accepted the religious tokens that Francis had sent and listened to the Saint's admonition with a humility that was unnatural for him. Francis' words, through the captain, seemed to have altered Ferrante's haughty attitude, as it did those of his counselors. Ferrante immediately rescinded his order to destroy the Hermit Friars' monasteries in the Calabrian region. He then issued an order empowering Francis to build monasteries anywhere in the Kingdom of Naples.

In a special personal message to the Saint, Ferrante invited him to erect one of his monasteries in the capital itself. At this special request, Francis sent two of his friars to take advantage of the King's offer. They were given a small church, Saints Louis and Martin, on the outskirts of Naples, where a magnificent basilica to St. Francis of Paola has been raised.

Francis' prediction that the Neapolitan branch of the House of Aragon would be destroyed became true within a few years. As already reported, Ferrante's second son, Cardinal Giovanni d'Aragona, died unexpectedly in 1485 at the age of twenty-five. Ferrante suppressed a revolt of his barons with such cruelty and bloodshed that it caused Pope Innocent VII to excommunicate him. The King then tried to create a schism in the Church. However, when Innocent died, Ferrante took steps to reconcile himself with the new Pope, Alexander VI.

In 1493, Charles VIII of France, as heir of the d'Anjous, former rulers of the Neapolitan Kingdom, threatened to invade Ferrante's realm and force him to abdicate. The Pope sided with Ferrante and refused to recognize Charles VIII's claims. Ferrante died of an apoplectic stroke on January 25, 1494, unmourned by his subjects.

His son, Alfonse II, the Duke of Calabria, became King. For his cruelty and immoral living, he was detested by his subjects even more than his unscrupulous father had been. However, when Charles VIII invaded Naples, Alfonso abdicated in favor of his son Ferdinand and fled to Sicily to the Abbey of Monreale, where he died one year later (1495). His son assumed the throne as Ferdinand II, but was forced to retreat to the island of Ischia, just off the Bay of Naples, while Charles VIII occupied the city. When the French finally left, he re-entered Naples, but died without heirs on October 5, 1496. During his short and hectic reign, he had proven himself a man of fairly good qualities.

On Ferdinand's death, the throne reverted to his uncle

Frederick, one of the sons of King Ferrante. However, unable to defend himself against Louis XII of France and Ferdinand V of Spain, both of whom claimed the Neapolitan throne, he abdicated and retired to France, where he died in 1504. With the death of Frederick, the Neapolitan branch of the House of Aragon became extinct, as Francis had predicted.

The great Spanish general, Gonsalvo de Cordova, finally forced the French out of the Kingdom of Naples and ruled it as the viceroy of Ferdinand V, King of Spain, surnamed "The Catholic." Gonsalvo, a devout Catholic and an admirer of St. Francis of Paola, repaired the damage done to the Hermit Friars' monasteries and re-established their monastery of Castellamare. Thus did the humble Servant of God achieve his purpose in his native land.

Chapter 12

FRANCIS AND THE KING
OF FRANCE

Louis XI, the King who united France into one nation and became the most powerful monarch in the world by his brilliance and political chicanery, in March of 1480—when at the height of his power—suffered a stroke that paralyzed him and affected his speech. He was the rebellious son of Charles VII, who had been crowned at Rheims, thanks to Joan of Arc's defeat of the English.

Confined to his castle at Plessis les Tours, Louis sought desperately a cure for his affliction. The leading physicians and miracle workers of Europe, religious and otherwise, were brought to his court, but to no avail. The unfortunate King grew steadily worse and more disheartened, although he continued to rule with an iron hand.

Finally, about two years after he had suffered his stroke, Louis learned through a courtier, Jean Moreau, of the miraculous cures produced by a holy hermit in far-away Calabria. Moreau, engaged in commercial ventures, had heard about Francis of Paola through a Matthew Coppola, a Neapolitan merchant, whose previously sterile wife gave him a child after she had been blessed by the Calabrian Miracle Worker. The King had Coppola summoned to his palace at Plessis les Tours, and, after questioning him at length, decided to send his chief steward, Guynot de Bussieres, to bring the Calabrian healer to France. De Bussieres, with Coppola, and a company of picked men, armed with a letter from the King to the Saint, started immediately for Naples and thence to Paterno, where the Saint was staying at the time.

On many occasions, beginning some twenty years before, the Saint had prophesied to his friars that there would come a time when he would go to a country whose language would be unknown to him and his language would be unknown to them. "But then, good Father," the friars would ask, "what use will it be to go among people who do not understand you and whom you cannot understand?" "Because," he would reply, "it will be the holy will of God."

Antonio Teramo di Figline, one of his intimate friends, recalled at one of the canonization hearings that about 1476, seven years before the request from the King of France, Francis had said to him: "My good friend, it will not be long before we shall have to leave for a distant land, where a language different from ours is spoken. It is the will of God that must be obeyed!"

These puzzling declarations of the Saint had no meaning to the Hermit Friars or his other followers until, to the astonishment of all, the delegation from the King of France arrived at Paterno. Only Francis himself, through his prophetic powers, saw nothing strange in receiving a letter from the King of France, asking him to come thither. In the letter, the King not only asked the Saint to attempt to cure his infirmity, but also offered him his sovereign protection and all possible help in establishing monasteries of his order in France.

Francis studied the King's letter and listened to the entreaties of de Bussieres and Coppola. However, the Saint did not feel that this was a call from God, but a call from a frightened monarch who wanted to save himself. This, Francis felt, was not enough to satisfy his own conscience, so he very politely but firmly turned down the King's invitation. De Bussieres, shocked by Francis' reaction to the urgent request of Europe's most powerful ruler, hurried to relay to Louis the Hermit Saint's flat rejection of his invitation. King Louis conferred with his ministers on the best way of getting this obstinate Calabrian wonder worker to change his mind. They felt that the most effective approach would be through Ferrante, the King of Naples, who had been allied with Louis and the de Medicis in recent wars against the Pope. Ferrante was reluctant to get involved because of the way he had scorned Francis' warnings about the Turks and his later arrogant actions against the Saint, which forced him to humiliate himself before his people by countermanding his orders to capture the Saint and destroy his monasteries. It was a hard pill for the vain King to swallow, but he dared not disappoint the powerful King of France. After due discussion with his ministers, most of whom despised the humble Hermit Saint as an imposter and troublemaker, Ferrante wrote Francis a letter couched in conciliatory language, begging him in behalf of his country and its people to agree to go to France.

De Bussieres, fully convinced that the letter from the Neapolitan King, Francis' monarch, would break down the Saint's objections, hurried to Paola where the Saint was at the moment. Francis received him with due courtesy and friendliness and read the letter from Ferrante. Without showing any emotions, he again told the French emissary, much as he regretted it, that unfortunately he could not accept the invitation. He pointed out that he was now sixty-five years of age, that the journey would be long and arduous, and that he lived such an austere, self-mortifying existence that he would not fit into the pomp and luxurious life in a court such as that of the most powerful monarch in the world. Francis also insisted that his powers had been greatly exaggerated and that he was not such a wonder worker as the King had been led to believe. Furthermore, he had to look after his monasteries in Italy. Much as he disliked to say no, he told de Bussieres, he simply was not in position to undertake the journey. De Bussieres, completely frustrated by the Saint's adamant stand, rushed back to Ferrante's court and reported that the Neapolitan monarch's letter did not change the Saint's attitude. Ferrante, who, after his experiences with Francis, had become fearful of the Calabrian Miracle Man, did not dare to try to use his royal prerogatives to force him to accept King

Louis' request. After another discussion with his ministers, it was decided to approach Pope Sixtus IV and have him try to break down the Saint's resistance. This had to be handled with great skill, for Ferrante and the King of France (along with the de Medicis) had been warring with the Pope and his allies for some time. The King of Naples relayed his recommendation to King Louis at Plessis les Tours. Despite his helplessness and his hostile feeling toward the Pope, King Louis ordered his ambassador at the Holy See, Marshal Jean Beaudricourt, to ask the Pope to use his influence in getting the stubborn Calabrian to accept the King of France's invitation.

The Pope, who, for reasons beneficial to the Church and its clergy, wanted the cooperation of this powerful monarch, addressed not one but two letters to the Holy Man of Paola, asking him to overcome whatever reluctance he had and—in the interest of the Church and the Christian world—to accept as expeditiously as possible the King's invitation. One of the Pope's letters is preserved in the monastery at Tours.

The Pope's communications had the desired effect, for Francis interpreted them as the will of God. He accepted them from de Bussieres without a word. So, after seven months of one-sided activities, the Saint prepared to take leave of his native Calabria, sadly aware, through his prophetic powers, that he would never return. Sixtus had asked him to pass through Rome so that he could confer on him his Papal blessings. De Bussieres wanted Francis to go with him on the French galley that was docked at Naples, offering to take him to Rome before moving on to France. But the Saint turned down the offer, telling de Bussieres that he had many arrangements to make before he could leave. He advised him to go on to Naples and that he would join him there at the earliest possible moment. De Bussieres, anxious to please his monarch, was disappointed, but he had learned not to try to force Francis to do anything that was inconsistent with his inner feelings, so he proceeded to Naples without him.

As indicated, Francis was fully aware that this would be his last sight of his beloved Calabria and that he could not leave until he was sure that all things were in order concerning his primary mission on earth. Furthermore, he felt great sorrow in having to leave people to whom he had devoted so much time, thought, and work, all of whom were cherished friends and devoted followers.

Paolo della Porta, of Paterno, a long-time follower, came to him with tears in his eyes to bid farewell. He asked: "Good father, now that we must part, can you leave me a small memento to remember you by?" The Saint, deeply moved, replied: "Dear brother, let the grace of Jesus Christ be with you forever, for this is the greatest and most precious gift." Thus saying, he withdrew from his pouch a small loaf of bread, obviously intended for his own use on his journey, and gave it to him. Paolo took the loaf with great joy and, when he got home, stored it away in a special place as a religious relic. It remained in that special place for five years, exuding a strange but pleasant odor. Then a famine struck Calabria, and Paolo's family found itself without food. Paolo thought of the small loaf that the Saint had left him. When he examined it, it turned out to be as fresh as the day the Miracle Worker had given it to him five years before. With some misgivings, he decided to use it as food for his family, who had had no nourishment for three days. It turned out to be more than enough to satisfy the hunger of the seven members of his family and had a delicious flavor. This was the final miraculous memento of the Holy Man's eternal charity on leaving Paterno.

Francis' parents, of course, had long since passed to their reward. The only close relative he had in Calabria was his sister, Brigida, with her five children. She was overcome with grief when she was told that Francis was leaving his native Calabria for France. She rushed to him with tears in her eyes. Weeping, she begged him to leave her a personal memento. The Saint consoled her, saying: "Dear Sister, in Charity, resign yourself to what must be. I promise to remember you every day before God in my prayers." Brigida, though somewhat comforted by her brother's promise, nevertheless wanted some personal token from him. Francis reached into his mouth and, without the slightest effort or show of pain, pulled out one of his molars and handed it to her, saying: "Very well then, keep this in memory of me." The molar is now among the Saint's relics in the monastery in Paola. It is split in half. Years after the Saint's passing, a woman who led a sinful life, to atone for her sins, visited the chapel where the tooth was on display. While in deep prayer she impulsively snatched the tooth and kissed it. When her lips touched the relic, it split in half. The woman was shocked by what occurred. When she had recovered, she sought out one of the priests, confessed her misdeeds and consecrated herself to a life of prayer, penance, and good works.

Uppermost in Francis' mind and heart was the effect that his departure would have on his order and the monasteries he had established throughout Calabria, Sicily and the Neapolitan Kingdom. Before he took leave of his brother hermits, he wanted to make certain that they would continue to promote the Order throughout the Italian peninsula, follow faithfully the simple rules he had laid down, and carry out temporal and spiritual works of charity among the poor, the helpless and the oppressed, without fear of those in authority. He named his most dedicated and competent hermit priest, Father Paolo Rendacio of Paterno, as vicar general of all the existing monasteries, with instructions to continue to build other monasteries on the Italian peninsula. He requested Father Rendacio to distribute the following personal message to all superiors, priests and brothers, in all monasteries:

"Sons of mine, whom I so love in the charity of Jesus Christ, I am separating myself from you to go to France. I have been commanded to do this by God, through His Vicar, the Pope in Rome! Hear the recommendations that I, as your father in Jesus Christ and as your legitimate superior, leave

with you. Love above all else our merciful Father in Heaven, and serve Him with all your strength and purity of heart. Maintain always charity among yourselves and with all other priests and brothers of the Order residing elsewhere.

"Maintain and mortify your members with a salutary and discreet penance, which will not permit you to fall victim to the insidious lures of the Devil, who cannot triumph except over those who are slothful and negligent. In the trials and temptations we face regularly in our daily lives, help one another and maintain with good heart the demands of your religious beliefs and commitments because in this way you will fulfill, as the Apostle says, the law of Jesus Christ.

"Obey with humility your superiors, for obedience is the backbone of faith. Each one of you must be sympathetic to the weaknesses and failings of others. I exhort you to persevere in your holy vocation, to which the Lord has so obviously called you, keeping in mind that the crown of salvation is won only by those who persevere, and that it is vain to begin a good action unless you bring it to full completion. Maintain yourselves with holy emulation on the path of virtue, which I have so ardently pursued, particularly in the practice of charity, humility and patience. I urge you to pray constantly to God for the exhaltation of His Holy Church and its followers, and for the steady growth of our small congregation.

"From what I have seen and heard about our friars, I have great faith in them. They seem not to need other guidance than that of their ordinaries. Nevertheless, to increase the value of obedience, and so that our activities will progress to proper order, I appoint Father Paul of Paterno as vicar general. He will be the superintendent over all monasteries, and you must obey him as if he were me in person. Those of you who are superiors, I ask you with all my heart diligently to practice cooperative charity. One superior must not interfere with the affairs of another. Everyone of you must love sincerely every priest and brother under your care and make certain that they are provided with all necessities, both spiritual and temporal.

"Make certain that they follow with conscientious care and

devotion the rules that I have issued. Write to me often, send-ing me news of yourselves and how our monasteries are pro-gressing. You will keep me informed on all those who will put on our holy habit, letting me know the exact number and the condition and background of each. Educate them with all diligence, impressing on them the true value of religious per-fection. You will forward such communications through the Ambassador of the Christian King [Louis XI] who is sta-tioned in Rome.

"These are, my dear ones, the paternal instructions I leave you in writing as a remembrance and a guide. I humbly ask that they be read once a week in a general meeting so that they will not be forgotten and as a continuous proof of your concern for spiritual perfection. They are also to remind you to include me in your prayers to God, Who is always among you, and Who will accompany me with His divine grace! Good-bye, my priests and brothers! We shall never again see each other on earth! May the Good Lord unite us in Heaven!"

With a great show of affection, Francis then embraced and exchanged the kiss of peace with every priest and brother present, and each went back sadly to his work as the Saint, equally sad, proceeded to make final prepara-tions for his historic journey.

Chapter 13

EN ROUTE TO NAPLES

Having completed all arrangements that his plans for the future of his order in his native land would be carried out according to his wishes, and having taken leave of all his followers, relatives and friends, Francis left Paola in the early part of February, 1483, on the first leg of his long journey—the trip to Naples. His companions were Father Otranto, Father Cadurio and his nephew, Brother Nicola D'Alessio. He was sixty-seven years of age at the time. The four pilgrims were accompanied by a small donkey called Martinello. They had no baggage, only small pouches swung over their shoulders or hanging at their sides. They were all clothed in the same simple maroon tunic and hood, with a cord around the waist; because it was cold, they wore simple open sandals on their feet and each carried a long staff. When any one of them became too tired, he would ride Martinello for a while.

The news of the Saint's departure for France had spread throughout Calabria, and people crowded the roadside, in silent sadness, to watch the little party pass. Many had witnessed some of the Saint's miracles or had been recipients of his charity and blessing. They watched with tears in their eyes, for they sensed that they would never see him again. The word had spread also through the Basilicata and Campania regions, and here too the people watched with reverential respect as the travelers went by.

They visited the monasteries at Corigliano and Spezzano on the east side of Calabria and went on through Castrovillari, an ancient Calabrian city near the Basilicata border. This town was built by the Greeks and there they still celebrated Mass in Greek at the time of the Saint. They then proceeded to Morano Calabro, where, it is said, they stayed at the Taverna della Bianca (Bianca's Tavern) near the Chapel of Sanita' (Health).

When they reached Mount Pollino, on the Calabria-Basilicata border, the Saint climbed to the top of one of its peaks, which gave him a panoramic view of the Calabrian countryside that he so loved and which he knew he would never see again. With tears in his eyes, Francis lifted his arms to heaven and called down God's blessing on this beautiful land of lakes and green fields and forests. The rock on which he stood so sadly and for so long retained the impression of his feet. Later the inhabitants of the area, some of whom had watched Francis take his long farewell look at his native land, discovered the impressions and the spot became a place of veneration and prayer.

Years later, one of his hermit friars from Morano Calabro cut out the stone and carried it to Rome, where it was placed in the Minimi Collégio dei Monti (College of the Mountains). However, Troiano Spinelli, the Prince of Scalea and Lord of Merano, demanded that the famous stone be returned. A section of the stone containing one footprint was returned and placed in a private chapel. Later it was transferred to the Church of St. Bernardino, near Merano. Today, in the Church of Mary Magdalene in Rome there remains the impression of the other foot.

When the four pilgrims reached Castelluccio, in the province of Potenza, Basilicata, they were tired and thirsty. Francis approached a man standing in front of his home and asked if he would fill a small cup with wine. The man, much disturbed, confessed to the Saint: "I would most gladly fulfill your wish, but my barrel has been empty for many days. There is not a drop of wine in it." The Saint, moved by the man's embarrassment, told him: "Brother mine, in charity I suggest that you go to your barrel and turn on the spigot. You will find that it is full of wine!" The man, quite puzzled and certain that the barrel was empty, decided to humor the pilgrims. He walked over to the barrel and turned it on and was stunned to find it full. He quickly filled the Saint's cup and ran back to the four hermits. Kneeling, he thanked Francis profusely for the miracle. The people who had observed the four pilgrims coming into the town soon learned of the miracle and rushed to see the Miracle Worker, watching him with reverence and wonder—some asking for his blessing. It was with great difficulty that the four could resume their journey to Naples.

When they reached Lauria, still in the province of Potenza, there occurred one of his most renowned miracles. Martinello, the faithful little donkey, had worn away his shoes and was walking with difficulty. When the group came to the door of a blacksmith shop, Francis asked in the name of Jesus if the blacksmith would be kind enough to provide new shoes for the donkey. Evidently the blacksmith had not understood the gist of the Saint's request. After he had fitted Martinello with the shoes, he asked for money. Francis was taken aback and said to him apologetically: "Dear brother, I asked you this in charity because none of us has money to pay you. Rest assured that the blessed Jesus will recompense you generously for your act of charity." The blacksmith replied angrily: "I care little for your poverty. I have served you, and now I want my pay." Francis tried to pacify him, but the blacksmith only became more infuriated, heaping curses on the four and insisting on being paid immediately. Seeing that he could not appease him, the Saint calmly said to the donkey: "Martinello, this man does not want to be charitable, and we do not have the money with which to pay him. Give him back his shoes!" Martinello, obeying his master, shook his hoofs and off dropped the four shoes! At the sight, the blacksmith became speechless. Humiliated and repentant, he dropped to his knees and begged the Saint for forgiveness, offering to renail the shoes on Martinello for nothing. But Francis sternly refused the offer and went on to the next town, Lagonegro, where he found a blacksmith who gladly shod Martinello as an act of charity and reverence.

The next day, the four reached Polla (the ancient Roman city of Forum Popilii) where they were greeted by a pious and charitable couple who gladly welcomed them into their home and fed them the simple food they requested. The couple was deeply impressed by the Saint's conversation and begged him to remain longer. He told them that this was impossible, so they asked him for something to remember his visit. Anxious to please this generous couple, the Saint reached into the fireplace, pulled out a piece of burning coal, and on one of the walls of the room he drew a sketch of himself. Turning to them he said: "There. That is all that I can leave you!" This drawing was revered for many years until one day, it disappeared mysteriously and no one ever knew why.

In the meantime, de Bussieres with two Neapolitan nobles selected by King Ferrante, Camillo Pandone and Cesare di Gennaro, went to Salerno to meet the famous Hermit. Salerno is some thirty-five miles south of Naples. When Francis and his companions appeared on the road to Salerno, the citizens rushed out with great enthusiasm to greet them, many kissing their hands or the folds of their tunics. They were led through an applauding crowd to the home of the Capograssos, a pious and ancient noble family, all of whose children had died in infancy. After they had fed them and made the Saint and his companions comfortable, they told Francis the reason for their unhappiness. Full of compassion, Francis promised to pray for them. To comfort them, he said: "Do not despair, for the Lord will give you other children, who shall live and carry on your family. But do not forget to baptize the first one Francesco Maria. To the others you can give any name you wish, provided that in all instances you will always add that of the Virgin Mother of God." Soon the Saint's prophecy was realized and the happy couple faithfully carried out their promise. Two and a half centuries later Monsignor Giuseppe Maria Perrimezzi, author of a two-volume life of the Saint (1713), reported that there lived many descendants of the Capograsso family and that they were held in high esteem and widely honored by the people of Salerno.

The Capograsso house in which the Saint and his companions were lodged, Perrimezzi further reports, was at the time he wrote (1713) owned by the Carrara family. In the room in which Francis had slept, the Capograssos had built a small altar in a recess in the wall, on which stood a statue of the Saint. The family prayed in front of this statue regularly.

The next day, in the company of de Bussieres and the two Neapolitan courtiers, the party resumed its journey toward Naples. When they passed through the Catena Gate, Francis pointed to the ancient Church of Saint Bernardino, telling his hermits that in time a monastery of the Order would be erected next to it. Nine years after his death, this prediction became a reality. In 1516, Roberto Sanseverino, Prince of Salerno, with the ready approval of the Salerno Senate, offered St. Francis' Minimi the church and additional ground to build a monastery to commemorate the Saint's visit to the city.

The next day at Cava dei Tirreni, a few miles north of Salerno, the travelers came to a place where a new church, a church to the Madonna dell' Olmo (Our Lady of the Elm), was about to be constructed. The Saint was asked to preside over the ceremony of laying the cornerstone. He gladly agreed. He also prophesied that within a century, his Hermits would erect a sanctuary there. In 1581, through a special arrangement between the Congregation of the Holy Name of Jesus—who owned the Church of Our Lady of the Elm—the Minimi, with the approval of the Pope, erected such a sanctuary.

At Cava, where he performed several cures and other miracles, Francis was approached by another noble couple, the de Curtis, who were also without heir. He assured them, as he had the Capograssos, that God would grant them a son.

In remembrance of the Saint's visit, a tablet was placed over the door of the church, reading: "To the new Miracle

Worker, St. Francis of Paola, who, on his way to France, while passing through this fortunate city, laid the first stone of this temple being built by the Confraternity of Jesus, prophesying that one day it would also include the brothers of his Order, which became true many years later, in the year 1581, through the piety and generosity of the citizens and the Confraternity. On that occasion, he also predicted to Signor de Curtis, chairman of the Congregation, that a son would be born to him and his wife, who would be an illustrious member of the family and of his country. The wife, who was infirm, was made instantly well by a fruit sent her by the Saint, as he had cured other sick citizens. As a lasting memorial the said Confraternity has erected this tablet in 1634."

The historian, Adinolfi, in a history of Cava written in 1848, relates that in the Church of Benincasa in Vietri, between Salerno and Cava dei Terreni, there is a picture of the Saint made during his journey through Salerno in 1483. It is said that the Capograssos had secretly engaged an amateur painter to make a portrait of the Saint while he was eating in their home. Francis, aware of the painter and that he was not competent enough to make a satisfactory likeness, gathered up the table cloth and pressed it against his body and face. When he removed it, the cloth had an impression of the Saint, somewhat similar to the image of Christ on the Holy Shroud of Turin. The portrait was kept in the Capograsso family until the plague of 1656 forced them to leave Salerno. They took the picture with them to the Church of Benincasa, where it was hung over the altar dedicated to St. Francis, presumably over the crypt in which their bodies were buried. Another historian, Polverino, however, claims that the incident occurred in the home of the de Curtis family of Cava dei Tirreni.

Chapter 14

FRANCIS IN NAPLES

On February 27, 1483, according to a consensus of historians, Francis and his companions reached the famous Capuana Gate, the most historic entrance into Naples.

Through this gate passed the first Aragonian king of Naples, Alfonso d'Aragon, exactly forty years before to the day, February 27, 1443—an interesting coincidence. Fifty-two years later, 1535, Charles the Fifth, the Holy Roman Emperor, entered through this gate into Naples amid wild cheers from the populace after his defeat of the great and much feared Turkish admiral, Barbarossa, at Tunis, where he destroyed most of the Turkish fleet that had devastated Mediterranean ports for years.

When he reached the famous gate, Francis and his hermits were greeted by a huge turnout of people, all eager to get a view of the celebrated Miracle Worker of Calabria. When the four travelers came into view, they were greeted enthusiastically and with great reverence by the Neapolitans. All municipal officials and leaders, headed by the Mayor of Naples, were at the gate. The welcoming committee included members of the nobility and of the merchant class. As the mayor was expressing his pleasure at meeting the Saint, a line of carriages, flanked by the royal guards, pulled up and out stepped the King of Naples himself, the proud Ferrante, and his three sons, Alfonso, the Duke of Calabria, Frederico, the Prince of Taranto, and Francis, the Duke of Sant' Angelo. They were accompanied by dignitaries of the court and city and the top echelon of the nobility. It was the most impressive assembly of people of importance in the history of Naples, and all to honor a humble, pious hermit following the simplest and most unpretentious of lives. The Saint and his companions seemed to accept this greeting calmly. Francis had learned to accept such things as a part of his mission in life. He obviously was pleased and showed every possible courtesy to the King and his nobles and courtiers.

As Francis walked slowly to the gate, two French and two Neapolitan nobles placed themselves at his side, walking with him toward the Capuana Gate. When they were almost there, King Ferrante (who two years before had ordered his arrest in chains) stepped forward and knelt before him and then embraced him. Francis accepted with deference and proper respect this unexpected display of affection and respect by the Neapolitan Monarch. The Saint thanked the King, his sons, his courtiers, and the people for this great demonstration of affection and respect.

The procession then moved through jammed streets toward the royal palace of Castel Nuovo. The going was difficult, for the people crowded the royal carriage in which Francis was riding, attempting to kiss the Saint's hands or at least to touch the folds of his garment. In addition to the packed crowds in the streets, scores of people were leaning out of windows and balconies, waving to the Saint. At one point Prince Frederick had to use troops to prevent Francis from being mobbed. Francis accepted this show of adulation as directed not to him but to God.

The procession finally reached the square in front of Castel Nuovo. The troops held back the people as the Saint and the royal party moved through the square and up the steps of the palace, Francis being flanked on one side by the envoy from King Louis XI of France and on the other by King Ferrante of Naples himself. At the top of the stair Queen Isabella, the Infanta (Princess), and the ladies of the court were waiting. When he reached the top of the stairs, they bowed and kissed his hands. Though this was a novel experience for the Saint, he accepted the honor with his usual humility and courtesy, which surprised the members of the court who had heretofore regarded him as an uncouth peasant.

One thing disturbed the Saint—the request from King Ferrante that he should stay in the palace, in a special room set aside and especially furnished for him. Francis would rather have stayed at the nearby monastery of his order, but after careful reflection, he decided that it would be in the best interest of his mission to accept the King's hospitality.

The castle in which the royal palace was located had been built in 1279 by Charles I of Anjou. It was outside of the walls of Naples and had been named "Castel Nuovo," to distinguish it from the old royal castle in Capuana. Castel Nuovo is a square castle with four towers, three on the entrance side facing the shore of the Gulf of Naples. It is in Gothic style. Its wide moat was filled with sea water. At the time of King Ferrante the castle was surrounded by orchards and vegetable plots. Later these were turned into impressive gardens. It was in the Castel Nuovo that Celestine V (Pietro da Morrone) abdicated the Papal Throne in 1294 after five months as Pope, returning to the life of a simple monk in the Order he had founded, the Benedictine Celestines. Ten days later, in this very same castle, the College of Cardinals elected Benedetto Gaetani Pope, as Boniface VIII.

Also from this Castle, Ludwig, the second son of Charles II, the Lame (King of Naples from 1285 to 1309), quit the royal court to become a Franciscan monk, dying as Bishop of Toulouse. Charles' successor was his first son, Robert I, who became known as "The Wise." He was an outstanding administrator and won the affection of his subjects. King Robert was a patron of the arts and sciences and gathered about him the most learned men of Europe. Giotto painted many murals in the Castle, and the King had soon collected the second largest library in Italy. He was the leader of the Italian Guelphs and was the first to try to unite the Italian principalities into one nation. Francesco Petrarca, the great poet, and Giovanni Boccaccio, author of the *Decammeron,* were frequent visitors to his court. After a memorable reign he died in 1343, deeply mourned not only by his own subjects but by the people of all Italy.

He was succeeded by his granddaughter, Joanna I, who reigned for thirty-nine years. She was a tyrant who strangled her husband. She was finally forced off the throne by her nobles, dying in obscurity in 1382. Whether the Saint was aware of the Castle's history is not known. Obviously, with his extraordinary powers, he must have sensed the palace's past and realized, as everyone knew at the time, that it was one of the most celebrated royal castles in Europe.

As was his habit, Francis periodically secluded himself in his room with his friars to pray and meditate. The room contained four richly furnished beds for the Saint and his three hermit friars and it was not far from King Ferrante's own royal bedchamber. The corrupt and cynical King, who just would not believe that men could really live such lives of strict self-denial and prayer, had arranged with his servants to cut peep holes—cleverly disguised as air vents—in the door to the Saint's room so that he could observe and hear what was happening without either the Saint or his companions being aware.

When he thought that the monks had retired for the night, Ferrante sneaked quietly down the hall and peeped into the room. What did he see? The three friars, overcome by weariness, were sound asleep on the floor next to the luxurious beds. In their midst was the Saint, floating in mid-air, his whole body glowing with light, hands clasped, praying fervently to God! The Monarch was stunned and stood watching, unable to move. After he had regained his composure, he quietly stole back to his room, convinced of the Saint's true holiness, which he had doubted for so long. The next time he saw Francis, he treated him with greater deference and listened to him with unaccustomed respect.

Francis was determined to prevail on Ferrante to change his ways, particularly as they related to the treatment of his subjects—in line with the letters he had sent him some years before. However, though the King listened attentively to the Saint's admonitions, he did not take too seriously the plea that he should be a Christian prince for the good of his own soul. The Saint, who could, of course, read the King's innermost thoughts, realized that if he were truly going to get him to change, he would have to perform an extraordinary miracle.

Many times the King had invited Francis to dine with him. But the Saint, with all due courtesy, had consistently declined, pointing out that he and his friars were committed to abstaining from practically all the foods found on the royal table. One day the King, while dining, ordered that a plate of fish that had been specially cooked for him be brought to the Saint. A page named Girolamo Cavaniglia obediently carried the dish to the Saint's room with the Monarch's compliments. Cavaniglia placed the plate of fish on the Saint's bed. Francis walked over to the bed and passed his right hand over the dish. In an instant, the fish were restored to life and started to move about. Then Francis said to the page, who stood there stunned by what he saw: "Carry these dear little animals back to the King and tell him how I restored life to these poor fish. In this way I want him to restore liberty to those unfortunates who are unjustly kept buried in his prisons!" The page, shaken by the miracle he had seen, rushed back to the King and delivered the Saint's blunt message. Ferrante was deeply shaken by the Saint's words. He ordered that the fish be put in silver vases and placed on a table where all could see them. They soon became a source of wonder and reverence in the royal court.

Ferrante decided that somehow he would make this stubborn Saint soften his stern attitude toward him. Earlier in his visit, the Saint had confided to Ferrante that he would have liked to build a monastery within the city of Naples. The King thought that this was an opportunity to win the Saint's gratitude and thereby make him less critical of the way he treated his subjects. He sent Francis a large vase filled with gold coins as his personal contribution toward building the proposed monastery. The Saint, sensing the Monarch's intention, refused the money, ordering that it be brought back to the King immediately with the message that he could not accept such an offering from a ruler who was so unjust, tyrannical and cynical. Then he went to the royal court and told Ferrante in a loud, stern voice: "Sire, your people are oppressed and made miserable by your government, which is an affront to God and mankind. Throughout your kingdom there is great suffering that is obvious and general. It is only the false reports from those who surround your throne that prevent you from hearing the cries of your oppressed subjects. Sire, remember that God placed the royal scepter in your hands— not for your self-enjoyment or to cause suffering—but to give you the means of doing good and bringing happiness to your subjects through the exercise of justice and charity. Do you ever give thought to the strict account the Lord will demand of you for all the injustices, acts of extortion, and cruelty that your ministers, in your name, are imposing on your poor, helpless people? Or do you believe that for kings there is no Hell? What would happen to your soul if at this moment you were to be summoned before the Divine Tribunal? This gold that you offered me to build a monastery in your capital city, this gold is not your gold; this is the blood of your people that has been squeezed out of them through your ruinous taxes and vicious tax collectors! I am speaking to you in a language that until now you have never heard, Sire, because, as your most faithful and obedient subject, I am not only concerned with the welfare of your people but also for the salvation of your soul. Therefore, in the name of God, I am now repeating that which I pointed out in the letters I wrote you sometime ago. If you do not amend your conduct quickly and do not improve your government, it will not be long before you and your throne will fall, and your family line be wiped out forever."

A speech such as this, so brutally frank and unequivocal, had never before been heard by courtiers in any court.

Stunned by the Saint's bold denunciation, the courtiers expected the apparently shocked King to vent his anger on the audacious Calabrian. Instead, the terrible tempered Ferrante responded in a quiet manner, telling the Saint that he had not been aware of the misery and oppression his people were suffering, that it was the fault of his ministers and emissaries, and that he would remedy these conditions as soon as possible. Francis, standing in front of Ferrante and angrily looking him in the face, dropped his staff and reached for one of the gold coins in the vase. Without difficulty he split it in two. Drops of blood dripped from the two halves, while the King and courtiers moved back aghast. "There is the blood of your subjects that cries for vengeance to God!" the Saint shouted. The Monarch, badly shaken, did not utter a word. When Ferrante had finally regained his composure, he again repeated his promise to reform his attitude and his government and he begged the Saint to appease God's anger against him through his prayers.

The haughty Neapolitan King seemed finally to have realized the awful spiritual power of the Calabrian Saint, the errors of his own ways, and the need to make proper amends.

One thing that Ferrante wanted before the Calabrian left his kingdom for France was to have a portrait of him. He asked one of the leading painters in his court to execute it. However, the Saint refused to pose for him, so he had to paint the portrait by observing him through the peepholes in the door that the King had used. The painting, which was an excellent likeness, is the one that in 1516, the Duke of Montaldo Uffugo, a nephew of Ferrante, donated to the Minimi Church of the Annunciation in the Naples area. It shows the Saint standing with his staff in hand, clothed in a tattered dark maroon tunic, with a gray background having a semicircle of thirteen stars.

Ferrante, much subdued and humble, again approached the Saint on his desire to build a monastery in Naples. This time, Francis accepted the offer and designed a monastery to be located on a hill near the shelter where some of his friars were then living and where he too stayed before his departure from Naples. The monastery was to be dedicated to Saints Louis and Martin. However, King Ferrante mildly objected, pointing out that this location was isolated and difficult to reach. The Saint said to him: "The day will come that this will be the most beautiful and widely traveled highway out of the city." This prediction came true when Pedro of Toledo built a magnificent palace just beyond the hill on which the monastery was located, attracting people from all over Europe.

In addition to miracles he had performed in Ferrante's Court, Francis performed other miracles in the Naples area that were reported at the various canonization hearings.

Margherita Coppola had been rendered helpless for many years by a severe asthmatic condition. At times she would find great difficulty in breathing, lapsing into semiconsciousness for days, unable to eat. She had heard of the Saint's many cures and decided to approach him. He listened patiently to her, then he blessed her and told her that she would be cured if she would eat a salad made of raw herbs seasoned with vinegar.

"But, dear Father, the doctors have all positively forbidden me never to eat anything seasoned with vinegar, and I know from experience that vinegar makes my condition much worse," she protested. The Holy Man soothed her and gave her two apples and a biscuit, and assured her: "In the name of Charity, do as I tell you, and do not worry about anything else. God will take care of you." When she got home, Margherita did as the Saint had instructed her. After she had eaten the salad seasoned with vinegar, she was immediately and completely cured. It is known from various sources that for the rest of her life she never again suffered from any form of asthma.

Margherita went to visit a friend named Marinella, who had a daughter suffering from running sores, like Lazarus in the New Testament. Margherita told of her miraculous cure by the Calabrian Saint and suggested that Marinella bring her unfortunate daughter to him. When they finally were able to talk to him, the Saint turned to Marinella, who was on her knees, and said: "If you really want God to grace your daughter, you must first restore the good name of your husband and that of your relative Antonia." Turning to the young girl, he handed her certain herbs, telling her to boil them and to use the water to wash herself. Shaken by the Saint's admonition, Marinella hurried home, apologized to her husband and to Antonia. Then she boiled the herbs. After her daughter had been washed with the water from the herbs, all her sores disappeared as if by magic.

A son of one of the Saint's most devoted noble friends in Spezzano, Iudicissa by name, who was in Naples, came to visit Francis and asked to accompany him on his trip to France. Iudicissa's father, a well-to-do and pious nobleman, had helped the Saint in building the monastery in the Spezzano Grande area. When the young man made his request, Francis tilted his head as if listening to some strange sound. He said to Iudicissa, "Do you hear anything?" The young man listened, then replied, "No." Francis said, "Very well, then come and listen here." Francis opened a window that faced onto the Gulf of Naples and asked again: "Now do you hear anything?" Surprised and puzzled, the young man said: "Yes, I do. It sounds like the bells of the church in Spezzano." "You are not mistaken," the Saint said. "These bells are tolling the death of your dear father. Accept the will of God, and return to your home right away so that you can put your family matters in order." Stricken by the news, which he did not doubt, Iudicissa left immediately for his home in Calabria. When he reached Spezzano, he found that the sad news was only too true.

Francis' stay in Naples, particularly in the palace, had produced some happy changes. The courtiers, who had been so scornful and suspicious before his coming, now bowed to him and paid him high respect, convinced by the miracles they had witnessed and by the way he had changed the attitude of Ferrante and his ministers. They saw him as a man of great holiness and compassion and completely devoid of fear.

Chapter 15

ROME—FIFTY-FOUR YEARS LATER

Two hectic weeks were spent at the Court of the Neapolitan King. At the urging of the French envoy, Guinot de Bussieres (anxious to fulfill his King's orders), Francis indicated in late February, 1483, that he was ready to continue on the second leg of his journey, the trip to Rome, the Eternal City.

Francis had passed through Rome with his parents in 1429, fifty-four years earlier. It was on their way to the shrine of his patron, St. Francis of Assisi, in the northeastern part of Umbria. In 1429 he did not see the Pope, but this time he would be in Rome at the request of the reigning Pontiff, Sixtus IV, and was to have private audiences with him. Sixtus was the Pope who had given complete and special approval to the Saint's organization and rules (except the one relating to the strict diet) and was very much interested in meeting Francis.

King Ferrante had personally selected a trireme galley that would take him to Rome. The galley, one of the best in the Naples harbor, was owned and commanded by Don Intraccato, in whom the King of Naples had special confidence. Ferrante arranged for his son, Federico, the Prince of Taranto, to accompany the Saint and his three hermit friars to the French royal castle at Plessis. He assigned Francesco Galeota, the court poet, and six other noble knights to guard Francis to his destination in France.

When the word spread through Naples that the Saint was leaving, he was met at the palace door by a delegation of citizens of all ranks. They paid him their deepest respects, thanking him for having come to Naples and for the many

117

miracles and acts of charity he had performed there. In wishing him a safe voyage, they asked that he not forget their city in his prayers. The Saint assured them that they and their city would always be in his prayers.

As they were boarding the galley at the wharf in front of Castel Nuovo, a huge crowd gathered along the shore. Just as the Saint came into view, they began to cheer and applaud. They bowed their heads as the Saint lifted his hand to bless them.

The Neapolitan King walked beside him as the party boarded the ship and stayed with him until the galley was ready to leave. Ferrante then said to Francis in a reverent tone: "Your leaving saddens me greatly, and I could not resign myself not to have you near me were I not certain that even far away you will not forget me or my kingdom. I do not have to remind you of the need of prayer for our people because I know and have seen proof of how dear to your heart is their welfare. Please assure the Most Christian King of France of the deep esteem I hold for him and the hopes I have for his early return to full health. Have a good trip and send us notice of your arrival in Tours."

Francis thanked the King for his warm hospitality and assured him that he would pray always to God for the religious and social welfare of his compatriots, whom he had always loved so dearly and would continue to love. He again urged the King to reform his government and the administration of justice and relieve the burdens that were crushing his subjects, among whom lived and worked his hermit friars, whom he recommended to the King's protection. The King, deeply moved, nodded consent to the Saint's final admonitions, then embraced him, kissing a fold of his garment. With the King ashore, the ship spread its sails and moved out into the Bay of Naples—the people crowding the shoreline, cheering loudly. The Saint in the stern took a last look at his native land, lifting his hands sadly to bless the throng.

The trip was uneventful until they were near Ostia, the ancient port of Rome at the mouth of the Tiber. For some unknown reason, the ship suddenly grounded on a sand bar just outside the port and could not be moved. To lighten it the captain ordered the jettisoning of cargo and furnishings—but nothing helped. The ship was stuck hard. The captain thought the ship lost and so advised the Saint. Francis went up to the bridge to survey the situation. He then asked the captain to have him rowed ashore. When he was on the ground, he went into a nearby briar thicket and knelt down in prayer. Suddenly the ship was afloat again and the sailors proceeded to dock it without further incident.

The travelers, when they reached Rome, were received by the French Ambassador, the Marshal of Baudricourt, who conducted the party to his embassy, where he had arranged to lodge Francis, his three hermit companions, the Prince of Taranto, Guinot de Bussieres, and the knights from the Neapolitan court. The palace was in the Trastevero area. It no longer exists. On the way to the French Ambassador's palace, the group passed a church. The Saint insisted that they enter and give thanks to the Almighty for the danger that they had escaped.

When they reached the embassy, the Saint and his friars were given a most cordial welcome. The French Ambassador was diffident at first, but after he had talked to Francis for a while, he became very friendly and keenly aware of the Hermit Saint's sincerity and humility.

The day after their arrival, Francis was summoned to a special audience with the Pope at the Vatican. Accompanied by the French Ambassador, the Prince of Taranto and his other companions, Francis made his way through the streets of Rome toward the Vatican. Word of the Miracle Worker from Calabria had spread throughout the city, and everywhere he was greeted by crowds, who watched him with deep respect and wonder as he passed by. The members of the Pope's staff treated the ragged Saint with great reverence. He was immediately ushered into the presence of Sixtus IV, who was seated on the Papal throne surrounded by his court. Francis and his three hermits, kneeling before the Pope, kissed his feet. After this act of respect, the Hermit Saint still on his knees, said:

"Most Blessed Father, I do not have the words to thank you with proper respect for the favor you have bestowed by approving and confirming, through your supreme apostolic authority, my simple religious views. I do not know how to thank your Holiness for the thoughtfulness that you have shown to me, so poor, so miserable, so unworthy to be in your presence or to kiss your sacred feet. May the Savior be blessed for inspiring your most charitable heart to confer on me this inestimable favor, which I, in my lowly state, never had hoped to receive. And here I am now before you, Most Blessed Father, ready to carry out whatever you will command. As obedient sons, my hermit companions and I, fully conscious of our religious commitments, have come at your call to renew our vows of obedience, chastity and poverty. I present your Holiness my three hermit companions, excellent examples of my humble congregation, and, in unison with them, I present to you all the other hermit friars who are in the monasteries in Calabria and in Sicily, as well as those who in the future will embrace our religious vows. Holy Father, I place my congregation completely under your care and humbly implore for all of us your Apostolic blessing!"

This speech, uttered before the whole Papal court by a simple and uneducated friar, surprised the cardinals and dignitaries present. The Pope, however, a man of wide understanding and sympathy, was deeply impressed. He rose from his throne and, as a sign of fatherly concern, embraced the Hermit Saint and then insisted that he sit beside him, telling him how deeply he had been moved by what he had said. Sixtus then explained to Francis how he wanted him to fulfill his mission to the most Christian King of France, for whose health the Pope was so concerned. Sixtus inquired about the state of his monasteries and other matters relating to the continuing progress of his congregation. He then dismissed the Saint and his companions; however, he told Francis that he would arrange a private audience so that they could more thoroughly explore the Saint's mission and various other subjects.

During his week-long stay in Rome, Francis had three separate audiences with the Pope, and he and his Hermit Friars visited the major churches and holy places in the Roman area. In his private audiences with the Pope, lasting three to four hours, the Saint sat in a chair next to the Roman Pontiff, who was constantly impressed by the Saint's simple eloquence, sincerity and frankness. There is reason to believe that Sixtus IV sought the Saint's views not only on religious matters, but also on politics and particularly the conflict then in progress between the Papal States and the Republic of Venice and her allies, a matter that Francis was to discuss with the King of France, as shown in letters now in the Vatican Archives.

However, the thought uppermost in Francis' mind in these private discussions with the Pope was obtaining Papal approval for the strict vegetarian fast practiced by his order. The strict abstinence he himself observed and had insisted that all his friars should follow was basic to their religious commitment. He pointed out to the Pope the importance for setting an example of self-denial, prayer and charity amidst the corruption and sensuality that prevailed throughout Italy and the world. The strict penitential way of life followed by his friars would not only help save their souls, but would be a constant reproach to the immorality and cynicism of society. Since he had now followed his prescribed diet for some fifty years, he pointed to himself as an example—now sixty-seven years old and in robust health.

Sixtus conceded that Francis and his friars should continue their strict diet, but he refused to confer Papal sanction on the practice. Disappointed but resigned to the Pope's decision, the Hermit Saint looked about him at the ecclesiastical dignitaries in the room. Among them was Cardinal Giuliano della Rovere, nephew of the Pope. Suddenly Francis, inspired by his prophetic powers, rose from his chair and, pointing his finger at the young cardinal, said: "Holy Father, there is the one who will concede what your Holiness is now denying me!"

Twenty years later the Saint's prophecy came true. The Pope's nephew, elevated to the Papacy as Julius II in 1503, two years later, in 1505 officially approved the perpetual Lenten fast as a requirement of the Saint's congregation.

Deeply impressed by Francis' sanctity and single-minded dedication to his mission and in his devotion to the Church, Pope Sixtus offered to ordain him a priest, despite the fact that he had no ecclesiastical schooling. The Pope pointed out that though he was self-taught, he was so completely and fully dedicated to God, self-mortification, prayer, prophecy and performing miracles, that this would more than fulfill the duties of the priesthood. The Pope's proposal stunned the Calabrian, and he dropped to his knees and, with tears in his eyes, begged him to recognize his lack of dignity and his ignorance and to permit him to remain what he wanted to be, the very least of all the members of his congregation. Sixtus IV, surprised by Francis' anguished plea, withdrew his proposal. However, he conferred on him the power to bless rosaries, candles, medals and other religious objects. He further conferred on him the Pontifical power to grant indulgences. These powers the Saint accepted willingly.

During his week's stay in Rome, many of the leading prelates of the Church, including cardinals, came to visit him at the French Embassy, asking for his advice and blessing. They were deeply impressed by the simplicity, humility and sincerity of the Calabrian. They came away more concerned with their religious obligations to their fellowmen.

Among those who came to visit the Saint was the famous Duke of Florence, Lorenzo de Medici, called the "Magnificent" in the history books, who was in Rome on business. After paying his personal respects to the Calabrian Holy Man, Lorenzo presented his son, Giovanni, who at the time was seven. He requested the Saint to bestow his blessing on his son, saying: "Giovannino, kiss the hand of the Saint!" On seeing the boy, Francis, suddenly aware through his prophetic powers of the boy's future greatness, embraced him and told him: "I shall be made a Saint when you are Pope!" And so it occurred. On March 2, 1513, Giovanni de Medici was elected Pope as Leo X. During the first year of his reign, he declared Francis a blessed, through a Papal decree. Six years later, May 1, 1519, at Leo X's urging, Francis was canonized a saint.

While wandering around Rome visiting the various churches, the Saint came to the hill by the Pincio, a small stream flowing into the Tiber. Standing on the ground that now is the modern Piazza di Spagna, he waved his hand toward the hill and said: "Not long from now, with the help of God, a monastery of our order will cover that hill." This prophecy came true twelve years later with the erection of the great Minimi Monastery of the Holy Trinity of the Mountains.

The French Ambassador, at the constant urging of his monarch, prevailed upon the Saint to resume his journey. Francis told him that he was ready to depart but wanted a final audience with the Pope, to receive the Papal Blessing for himself and his friars. The Saint, when he reached the Vatican, obtained an immediate audience with Sixtus. Prostrating himself at the feet of the Pontiff, he again assured him of his and his followers' complete devotion and loyalty and requested the Pope's final blessing. Sixtus told them, in the interest of the Church, to go to the French court and do what was possible to help the French King, pointing out that God was directing their steps. He said that he would pray fervently for the success of the mission and asked the friars to pray constantly for him and for the Church. Sixtus then gave them the Papal Blessing and told them to go in peace, assured that Almighty God would bring them safely to their destination.

On the way to the port of Ostia, the Saint was stopped by a man who was out of breath from running. It seems that his wife, a very pious woman, had gone to the French Embassy to collect some momento of the Saint. The only thing that was available was a handful of hay on which the Saint had slept. She took it happily and rushed home. When she showed it to her irreligious husband, he ridiculed her and profaned her belief. Scornfully he snatched the handful of hay from her. No sooner had he grasped the hay, than his arm became completely paralyzed. Repentant, he had rushed after the Saint. He begged him to restore the use of his arm. The Saint said: "Be assured, brother, and return to your home because you have nothing more to fear." As the Saint spoke, the arm of the frightened man was completely restored, and he went back to his wife, apologetic and repentant.

Francis and his companions, including the French envoy, de Bussieres, and the French and Neapolitan courtiers, continued their way to the wharf where the galley was docked.

Chapter 16

FROM OSTIA TO TOURS

When the Saint and his party reached Ostia and the ship to France, it was discovered that the tide had gone out and had left the ship moored high and dry. As de Bussieres reached the dock, the Captain gave him the bad news and told him that the tide was unpredictable and the ship might not be floated for hours. The Frenchman, irritated by further delays and knowing how anxiously his King was looking forward to meeting the Calabrian Miracle Worker, ordered the Captain and his crew to use every means possible to float the ship.

"The water has gone out with the tide," the Captain protested, "and all our efforts to float the galley are in vain." At this moment, Francis walked up and heard the Captain's complaint. He turned to the sailors and commanded: "In the name of Charity, brothers, measure the water again, because, with the help of God, it should prove sufficient." They measured again and discovered, to their surprise, that the water had risen six palms, enough to float the ship. They went aboard, and when they had raised their sails, the galley moved smoothly into the sea and headed toward France.

As the ship sailed through the Gulf of Genoa, some followers claim the Saint pointed to a hill visible beyond Genoa and predicted that a monastery of the Order would soon be built there. Twelve years later this prediction was realized. When they reached the Gulf of Lyons, a violent storm forced them to approach the nearest coast and cast anchor. Shortly after they had dropped anchor, a ship of Turkish pirates appeared in view and, despite the storm,

moved toward the Saint's ship with the intention of boarding it. When near enough, the pirates began to bombard it
with their cannon. The captain and the officials in great
fear came to the Saint for advice. Francis said to them:
"Brothers, raise the anchor and have no fear! With the
help of God, none of you will be hurt!" At that instant, the
pirate ship became immobile, and with a sudden favoring
wind from the tempest, the Neapolitan galley sailed away,
unharmed.

When the galley reached the port of Marseilles, it was
denied entry because of a terrible plague that was raging
all along the Mediterranean coast of France. The ship
sailed to the east along the coast, past the Island of
Hyeres, and entered the Bay of Bormes, landing at a port
called the Cape of the Dove. The Saint, who had remained
in his cabin in prayer and meditation with his three friars
during most of the trip, refused to go ashore until Father
Bernardino had heard his confession and given him abso-
lution. The Calabrian Holy Man feared that if he had not
been absolved of his sins before landing in France, he
would draw down the anger of God on the land in which
he was to carry out his apostolic mission.

Before going ashore at Bormes, Francis thanked the
Prince of Taranto, the Neapolitan knights, the ship's Captain and the crew for the courtesy and consideration they
had shown him and his companions, and gave each a small
blessed candle. Francis and his three hermit friars landed
with de Bussieres and Francesco Galeota, the poet-patri-
cian sent by King Ferrante to accompany the Saint to the
French Court. The Neapolitan Prince and his companions,
unable to land because of the plague, turned around and
headed back to Naples.

On the return trip, the Neapolitan galley ran into a
violent storm, which kept the crew and passengers fully
occupied. The storm continued through the night and the
next day. All those aboard were completely exhausted. In
desperation some invoked the assistance of the Saint they
had just left in France. One member of the rowing gang,

Philip Fabalengo, who despised the Saint, found a pair of sandals of the Calabrian under a bench. Shouting scornfully, "Here are the sandals of that damned friar, who could have saved me from my misery as a galley slave, but did not," he threw the sandals into the raging waves. No sooner had they landed in the water than the giant waves were miraculously calmed. The galley was able to reach Protevenere, near La Spezia, where necessary repairs were made; it then sailed back to Naples without further incident.

In the meantime, Francis and his companions were being refused entrance to Bormes because of the plague. De Bussieres requested entrance in the name of the King, but the guards at the gate, in accordance with their orders, refused entry. The Saint then came forward and said in a quiet voice: "In the name of Charity, brothers, let us enter, for God is with us. At his words, the guards, responding to some mysterious urge, threw open the gates and the Saint and his party entered.

Once inside the stricken city, the Saint looked for a church where they could thank God for the voyage so successfully completed and to prevail on Him to end this terrible plague that was ravaging the city. The church, dedicated to San Rocco, was then under repair. Some workers were having difficulty placing a heavy beam where it was intended. Francis walked over to them and touched the beam, telling it: "In charity, you must serve the house of God, without causing so much frustration to these good brothers." The beam became immediately light enough so that the workers, with minimum effort, were able to place it where it belonged.

The news of this miraculous act, witnessed by many individuals, spread throughout Bormes. The people rushed to greet the Saint as an angel sent by God to save their city. Soon the church was crowded with people, begging the Miracle Worker to free them from the awful pestilence. In response to their prayers, the Calabrian asked to be directed to the nearest hospital, which he found crowded with people suffering from the plague. Filled with compassion, the Saint made the Sign of the Cross over them, and they all were instantly cured! According to historians, the plague no longer affected the people of Bormes, and those affected from other areas who came to Bormes were also miraculously cured. The Saint's intercession continued to protect Bormes for centuries. It is reported that in 1835, some 300 years later, while a cholera epidemic was raging in southern France, the people of Bormes remained untouched.

Toulon, some twenty miles west of Bormes, was almost depopulated by the plague. Records indicate that during the months of July and August, the months when the plague was most virulent, there were no deaths reported in Bormes after the Saint had visited it. The people of Bormes, in gratitude to their benefactor, initiated devotions for his intercession. When the Saint was canonized in 1519, they erected a church in his honor. In the sixteenth century a monastery was built by the city for the Saint's congregation.

Francis remained only two days in Bormes, a guest of the governor. During that time he worked several miracles. One of the most memorable was restoring to life cooked fish that had been prepared for him by his host, unaware of the Saint's strict diet. People swarmed around the governor's palace to be near the Calabrian Miracle Worker, stripping off pieces of his tunic and hood. The Saint permitted them to do this, fully aware that God would renew his clothing as fast as it was being torn away. Spectators were amazed to see that after scores of people had torn away pieces from his hood and tunic, they both were still miraculously whole.

When Francis was ready to leave, the great crowd which had gathered before the governor's palace expressed their gratitude for the miraculous cure and asked to receive his blessings. Unable to make his way through the crowd, so closely packed in the square, and embarrassed by their adulation, the Saint decided to use his supernatural power of disappearing before their eyes. No door had opened and yet the Saint was no longer there, to the astonishment of all present. His puzzled companions found him waiting for them outside the walls, ready to resume their journey.

For charitable reasons he went to the city of Frejus, which was the bishop's see, where the pestilence was raging uncontrolled, killing scores of people. Frejus was the ancient Roman city of Foro Iulensis. When Francis entered through the Meous Gate, he found the city practically deserted. On his way to the cathedral, he encountered a woman and asked her why the city was so empty. "Oh, dear Father, do you not know of the plague that prevails? Almost half our citizens have already died, and of the remainder, some have left the city, and the others are rendered helpless by the plague," she told him. "Very well, then, you go tell the people that I am here to help them." The woman, surprised by his words but nevertheless sensing his unusual power, went to the center of the city and told the people about Francis. They reacted to the woman's story and rushed to the governor's palace where the Calabrian Saint stood. He made the Sign of the Cross over those who were afflicted, and they were made whole. The city was soon cleared of the pestilence.

The next day the Saint left, cheered by the grateful populace. In 1490, seven years later, the people of Frejus erected a church and a monastery, called Our Lady of Pity, in honor of the Calabrian Miracle Worker.

When Francis was canonized, the people of Frejus made him their patron saint, and every year, on the third Sunday after Easter, they celebrated a solemn feast honoring his coming and his meeting the woman at the cathedral. The Saint continues to protect the city. In 1720, when the southern coast of France was again devastated by a plague, the city of Frejus, thanks to his special protection, was spared.

While the Hermit was taking time out from his journey to the French court in order to perform miraculous cures and acts of charity in coastal cities, de Bussieres dispatched one of his trusted aides, Jean Moreau, to Louis XI, advising him that Francis had finally arrived in France and was on his way to his court. The King, overjoyed at the news, addressed a letter to the Council of Lyons, through which city the Saint had to pass, asking that a wagon litter be prepared for the sixty-seven year old Holy Man so that his trip to the palace could be speeded. The letter, dated February 24, 1483, was delivered by Rigault Dereille, one of the masters of ceremony in the King's household, who was to supervise and direct all necessary arrangements. The King also requested that he be kept informed of the Saint's progress through the various cities. In a second letter, dated March 27, 1483, the King stated that the Calabrian Hermit Saint be treated as if he were "Our Holy Father" (the Pope). Both of these letters are still extant.

Francis and his companions traveled from Frejus to Lyons on horseback. Along the way, the fame of the Saint preceded him, and the road was lined with people who, with wonder and reverence, watched him go by. The Saint, of course, blessed the onlookers as he rode along. He also insisted on taking time out for his periods of prayer and meditation, stopping when possible at churches by the wayside. They reached one village on the way to Lyons and stopped to ask for water. The villagers sadly told the Saint that they were suffering from a drought and at the moment had no water. On hearing this, Francis dismounted, turned his eyes to Heaven, prayed, and then struck the ground in front of him with his staff, and a spring burst forth on the spot, gushing clear, fresh water. The water also had curative power, it was discovered, especially against fevers. The miracle was reported by a goldsmith of Grenoble, who was present.

While in Grenoble, the Saint saw a church a short distance away which offered the seclusion he wanted in order to commit himself completely to prayer and meditation without being distracted. When he had been in the church for some time, de Bussieres and a merchant from the Provence region of France (along the Mediterranean) went into the church to remind him of the time. They could not see the Saint at the altar or anywhere else in the church. They made a thorough search and also called in other members of the party, but the Saint was nowhere to be found. De Bussieres was concerned. He feared that somehow the Calabrian Holy Man had taken flight. As the members of the group stood outside the church wondering what to do, the Saint appeared, serene and relaxed, obviously refreshed by his act of devotion. He offered no explanation for his disappearance. Evidently he had willed to become invisible to human eyes during his period of deep prayer, as he had done on occasions before.

The party remained one day in Lyons at the Inn of the Griffin. Claude de Rubis, one of the King's counselors, reported that the people of Lyons believed that God operated through the Calabrian Hermit. They referred to him as the "Holy Man," and considered themselves fortunate if they could touch his clothes, his staff, or other things he carried. His one-day stay at the Griffin Inn has been memorialized by a receipt for expenses paid by the King's representative, Jean Colombier, dated Wednesday, April 24, 1483, some three months after he had landed on French soil. Also, receipts still exist for apples and grapes purchased for the Saint by the King's representative.

Also remaining is the invitation to the Saint from Antoine Dupont, procurator general of Roanne, the capital of the Department of Loire, and also a receipt from Richard des Cortes, covering the toll paid for the Saint's crossing the bridge to the city. The party passed on through the cities of Nevers, Auxerre, and Orleans, which last, under the name of "Genabum," was destroyed by Julius Caesar, some fifty years before the coming of Christ, and rebuilt by Aurelian around 270, after whom it is named [Latin— *Aurelianus,* hence Orleans]. In Orleans he was a guest in the home of a pious citizen who lived on St. Catherine Street. When they arrived at Amboise, the Dauphin, who later became Charles VIII, greeted them and knelt before the Saint to receive his blessing. This was early in May,

1483. The Dauphin then led them to Tours on whose outskirts was the King's castle.

Chapter 17

FRANCIS AND THE KING OF FRANCE

Louis XI, son and heir of Charles VII, spent the happiest days of his youth in the Castle of Loches in the Touraine region of France; this was his father's castle near Amboise, which was kept as the family residence. In 1463, two years after he had been crowned king, he acquired a plot of land about two miles southwest of Tours, where he built a winter palace. It was a castle of simple design in the style of the period. He named it "le Plessis," which has become identified in history as "Plessis-les-Tours." As mentioned, his father was the man whom Joan of Arc helped make King of France by defeating the English in 1428. At that time Louis was only five years old. He himself had been crowned king on August 15, 1461, in Rheims, at the same cathedral in which his father had been crowned.

Louis, though a tyrant, was clear-thinking and forward-looking, with simple personal tastes. He was a champion of local political leaders and the merchant class. Because of a weak, sickly body, he was known as "The Spider" among his detractors. However, he was well-educated, a shrewd diplomat and statesman and, when health and the weather permitted him, regularly visited all parts of his kingdom. He reunited France and completed the reorganization of the government, which had been started by his great grandfather, Charles V, more than 100 years before. He also reorganized the army, avoided wars, and brought prosperity to his people, while increasing taxes, however. He was an absolute ruler, scorning the actions of the French Parliament. In 1480, his health had deteriorated so badly, that he locked himself in his chateau at

134 *Saint Francis of Paola*

Plessis, guarded by his most loyal followers, and refused to see anyone except his most trusted counselors and aides. As his illness progressed, he sought the help of the best physicians in Europe, and also that of astrologers and necromancers. Though weak and wracked with pain, he continued to rule France with great shrewdness and with an iron hand and to dominate European rulers, particularly the Italian. In March, 1480, when fifty-seven years of age, Louis XI suffered a stroke that left him paralyzed and impeded his speech. In 1482 he learned of the many miraculous cures performed by Francis, the Holy Man of Paola in far-away Calabria. As it has already been reported, he used every possible means, including the Apostolic powers of the Pope, to force the Calabrian Saint to come to his court. Now—May, 1483—more than a year after he had made his original request, the great Miracle Worker was at his gate, in the hands of his only son, the Dauphin.

When the people of Tours heard that the celebrated Calabrian was approaching, they, including political figures and representatives from all the parishes, went out to meet him. The shoving and pushing by the people trying to touch him threatened to crush him. The King's soldiers had to restrain the crowd and clear for the Saint a passage to the city square where political and clerical leaders of Tours were waiting to greet him as they would have the Pope, according to the King's orders.

The crippled King, in the meantime, had clothed himself in his most royal robes and, surrounded by palace guards, his chief counselors and the dignitaries of his court, went to the city square to welcome personally the humble Calabrian Hermit. When he finally stood in front of the Holy Man, the most powerful king of Europe dropped to his knees and, with deep humility and tears in his eyes, touching his tattered clothing, implored the Saint to cure him of his infirmities. Philippe de Commines, Louis XI's biographer, was present, but he did not quote verbatim Francis' reply in his *Memoires*. He merely states that the Saint, completely unawed by the royal presence, *"repondit ce que un sage homme devoit reprondre,"* ("Answered what a wise man should answer.") The Holy Man of Paola, who had cured so many desperately ill people of humbler station, knew from God that he was not to cure the most powerful man alive! However, the unlearned Calabrian knew that he could not tell Louis the truth and had to answer with prudence and compassion in order not to frighten or anger him. The Saint knew that whatever miracle he might have effected that would have saved the King physically would have condemned his soul to eternal punishment.

However, for Louis this was a moment of great joy; with his spirits uplifted, he walked bravely beside the Calabrian, happier than he had been for many days. He led him to quarters adjacent to his castle that had been furnished for Francis and his three hermit companions. The lodgings were in a building beside the castle gate, next to the Chapel of St. Matthias. This chapel, which was erected through the express order of Sixtus IV, issued March 29, 1482, one year before the visit of the Calabrian Miracle Worker, was designated as the parochial church for the King and his court. All traces of these buildings have disappeared, including the small Minimi Monastery and the granary that replaced Francis' cell.

After having escorted the Saint and his religious trio to their quarters, the King instructed Guynot de Bussieres, who had become thoroughly familiar with the Hermit's strict requirements and routine, and Peter Briconnet, the King's treasurer, to provide whatever the Hermit Friars requested. He also selected a faithful courtier to act as interpreter for Francis, who did not understand French. He was Ambrose Rambault, who became a very devoted follower of the Calabrian Holy Man, gaining his confidence and friendship. Louis Dony d'Attichy, Bishop of Rietz, in his biography of the Saint in France, has preserved a letter in which the Calabrian Saint, after the death of Louis, requested his son, Charles VIII, to provide Rambault with steady employment. The Saint's undated letter to Charles VIII is as follows:

"Sire: You remember the bearer of this letter, Ambrose Rambault, of your city of Tours, who, for the services rendered by him to your father (may the Lord help him) you had promised to take care of him. He has [rendered] and continues to render many vital services to our religion. Your late father assured me that he would continue to act as the interpreter of my Italian idiom, which he knows how to speak and write as well as Latin. Sire, if it will please you, will you as a favor to me and my religion, maintain him in whatever employment you may find him useful, thus making me beholden to your charity, obliging me to pray to God so that you will prosper. Sire, I pray that the Son of God will grant you a long and useful life. Your humble servant, Friar Francis of Paola."

When one of his financial representatives, Francis de Genas, stationed in the Langdoc region, insisted on paying Guynot de Bussieres, the King's majordomo, who had brought the Calabrian Saint to France, only half of his travel expenses, the King wrote him a blistering letter that indicated that his long illness had not affected his thinking or his imperial temper. The letter, dated May 15, 1483, reads as follows:

"Dear General, my majordomo of the Oaks, Guynot de Bussieres, who has brought the Holy Man to me, complains that you have denied him half of the money he spent for this purpose, amounting to 600 lire tornese, explaining that this was in accordance with my orders. This is not true. I have never issued such an order. Be assured that I am not happy over your action, and look well that you do not disobey me. When you receive this letter, you will see to it that he will be fully reimbursed for his expenses so that I will never hear further complaints on this matter. If this is not quickly done, I shall have no further need of your services. Also remember

that should you delay in carrying out my request, you will be turned over to the hands of Monsieur D'Alby. Beginning now and until I hear from Monsieur D'Alby that you have fulfilled my order, your pay and pension will be suspended. Written at Plessis-du-Parc, May 15, 1482."

The letter is signed simply and significantly *"Louis."* (The date shown in the above letter is according to the old calendar, which is one year behind the modern calendar.)

Louis saw the Calabrian Holy Man at least once each day, always asking him to cure him, and the Saint, with great tact, managed to appease the insistent Monarch. In order to ingratiate himself more with the Humble Friar, the confused King wrote a second letter to General de Genas on June 29, 1482, requesting some special fruit and vegetables for the Saint. It reads:

"Dear General: I pray you to send me lemons and sweet oranges, moscadelle pears and parsnips. All these are needed by the Holy Man, who eats neither meat nor fish. In this way you will do me a great favor. Written at Clery, June 29, 1483. Louis."

Once established in his quarters, and finding himself and his brother friars among people whom they could not understand, Francis, moved by a feeling of homesickness, wrote to his sovereign, King Ferrante of Naples, advising of his arrival and his meeting with the King. He also told him that he was praying regularly for him and the welfare of his royal family and kingdom. The letter is preserved in the Monastery of St. Louis in Naples. It was delivered by Francesco Galeota, the Neapolitan court poet and knight, when he returned to Ferrante's court, along with a small blessed relic which is still preserved in Naples. The Calabrian Holy Man's letter to his King reads as follows:

"Sire: According to the mandate of the Holy See and your Majesty, I am with the King of France in his castle at Plessis.

*I have found a King of great good will in rendering proper
homage to God, to establish the lasting peace in your Kingdom that your Majesty has desired with great passion, and to
take measures to drive out the enemies of God and of the
Church in Italy. I pray daily to God that he favor the divine
wishes of your Majesty, and I shall not miss any opportuni-
ties to prevail on the King to fulfill this commitment, to
which has been given such an auspicious beginning. I do not
let a day pass without praying to God to preserve the health
and prosperity of Your Majesty and that of your most serene
Queen, your wife, the illustrious Duke of Calabria, your son,
and all of your subjects, for whom I pray for many benefits
under your reign. I also pray that you will continue to reaf-
firm your dedication to God and true justice to your subjects,
for these are the two pillars on which rest the greatness of
empires and monarchies. Toward this end I ask God for an
abundance of heavenly grace. I remain Your most obedient
servant, the poor Minimi brother, Francis of Paola, from
Plessis, May 16, 1482."*

On August 18, 1483 (according to the modern calendar), Ferrante replied:

*"Our dearest, most venerable and pious Father, I have re-
ceived your letter of May 16 from the hand of Francesco
Galeota, which carried so much consolation that I cannot
properly express my gratitude in a letter. Considering
what great concern you hold for our honor, our well-being
and the well-being of our subjects, which we could not be enjoying except through the holiness of your life and your
singular virtues, we pray that you will pursue with God and
with men peace for our poor Italy, and force the enemy of
our Religion and the Church out of its boundaries. However,
what we consider most urgent at the moment is that the most
Christian King (whom we regard as our father) should be
cured of his infirmity, a favor that you alone can obtain
through God. We pray you then, with all the love that we feel
for you, that through your saintly prayers, you will solicit the*

Creator to restore the King's health. We are certain that, because of your complete commitment, God will heed your prayers and make His Majesty whole again, whom, as we have indicated, we consider our Father, and are as concerned over his health as we would be with our own. In regard to peace in Italy, we leave it to your piety and goodness. We know that you are revered by all the people here. They regard you as a loving Father, and feel deeply your absence. In fact, the most Christian King must know for certainty, that if it were not for the concern for his royal person, neither I nor any of my subjects would have permitted you to leave our kingdom. We were convinced that your very shadow protects us from even the most sinister threats. We now realize, because you are so far away, the happiness and consolation we derived from your inspiring presence. But, because of our deep affection for the person of the most Christian King of France, we could not deny what, with such earnestness, he requested. We pray each day to God for the preservation of the good Prince, and again beg you to do whatever you can to make him whole.

"We have received with great happiness and affection the relic you sent us, and we thank you in behalf of the most serene Queen, our dear consort, the illustrious Prince of Calabria, our son, and all our subjects. We ask you to recommend us to God in your prayers. On our part we will pray to our Lord, that he make you a saint and fulfill your most holy desires. Given in the New Castle of Naples, August 18, 1482. King Ferdinand."

Francis was constantly concerned with the progress of his congregation and of his monasteries in Italy, particularly in Calabria. His concern is indicated in a letter he wrote to the Princess Eleanor Piccolomini, of Bisignano, in the Province of Cosenza, some twenty miles northeast of the city of Cosenza. The letter reads:

"Most serene Princess: I am deeply grateful for your kindness toward God and your house of the Holy Trinity, as well

as for our monasteries established within your principality. I have received a bull from our Holy Father, The Pope, which I permitted to be distributed, conferring [a] plenary indulgence once a year on brothers, procurators, oblates and nuns in our order. However, to share in these indulgences, I appoint the serene Prince, your husband, and your serenity, procurators of the Monastery of the Holy Trinity at Corigliano and in other locations, so that through your persons you can make certain that our constitution and religious requirements are properly observed. Love God above all human beings and neighbors, and keep Jesus Christ in your thoughts always, who in His compassion will grant to you and to your children and principality a worthy life. God be with you. Tours, June 6, 1482. Of your Excellency an unworthy servant, Brother Francis of Paola, a poor hermit."

(Note: The letters were dated according to the old calendar. The modern calendar makes it a year later.)

Chapter 18

THE KING TEMPTS THE SAINT

As Louis XI became weaker, he also became more and more recluse. However, he wanted to maintain the appearance of strength and robust health for his subjects and the world at large. He issued orders and wielded his authority with vigor and arbitrary abandon and indulged in extravagances that were widely publicized. His biographer, de Commines, reports that, as his illness progressed, contrary to his simple tastes in the past, he devoted more and more attention to clothing himself in costly raiments, made of the finest velvet and silk, and embellished with gold and precious stones.

To strike fear and respect, he would dismiss officials out of hand for the slightest deviation from his orders, would reduce or cancel pensions, and would visit the severest punishments on those who violated rules of court or the law of the country. To impress other nations, he would add more personnel at French embassies and send his courtiers to all parts of Europe to purchase prize horses and hunting dogs, rare animals and precious stones. He wanted to be certain that those who might conspire against him—had they known the true state of his health—would be kept in complete ignorance.

Though some writers have tried to create the impression that Louis XI was a freethinker and even an unbeliever, the records show that he was a practicing Christian, receiving the Sacraments regularly and following the Church's laws, except when they conflicted with political expediency. Throughout his kingdom, he encouraged processions and other public religious activities, subsidized pious foundations and programs, and fostered the collection of relics of the saints in the churches.

The Pope, basing his opinion on reports that he received, saw him as the most Christian of kings and was especially concerned that he should continue to live and reign as an example to the other rulers of the day. This provided a tremendous problem for the Calabrian Saint, being aware that the Creator did not want the French King cured, but wanted him to become a firm believer and a true Christian.

The Monarch came every day to visit the "Good Man," as he referred to the Hermit from Calabria. When he came into the Saint's presence, he would kneel in deep humility, according to observers, including Louise Poupillart, wife of the nobleman Felix Martel, who gave testimony on this point at the canonization hearings at Tours.

Down on his knees, the King of France pleaded with the Saint to cure him, prayed long and earnestly with him, and made all sorts of promises. However, Francis knew that the King's piety was not from the heart. The Calabrian would constantly point out to the wretched Monarch that his health and his life, like those of all mortals, was in the hands of God, and that God had numbered everyone's days. He told the King that he had to put his conscience and his life in order, and the rest would be the will of the Heavenly Father.

After the Saint had failed to restore his health, Louis became suspicious. He suspected that those who were plotting against him had somehow bribed the Calabrian and that he was deliberately permitting him to die so that he would be rewarded by his successors. However, the suspicious King did not want to antagonize the Saint, so he decided to turn directly to the Pope and let him use his divine office to pressure the Calabrian to cure him. The letter of the Pope in answer to that from Louis XI has been preserved in the Vatican. It is in Latin, and in it was enclosed two "briefs" to be transmitted to Francis. The first was an order that he should ask God to cure the French

Monarch and the other (which was to be delivered to the
Calabrian Miracle Worker at the discretion of the King)
threatened possible excommunication should Francis hold
back his miraculous powers in case some enemies of the
King had convinced him otherwise. Only the text of the
first still exists in the *Liber Brevium (The Book of Briefs)* at
the Vatican. It reads:

*"Dearest son, regards. We have heard with great pleasure
of your safe arrival into the presence of his royal Majesty. We
are most desirable that his Majesty receive every advantage
from your visit such as he had hoped for. We desire and request, under saintly obedience that, with all due care, zeal
and diligence, you obtain the cure of his Majesty, praying
God to be expedient, regardless of any suggestions to the
contrary that others may have made to you. We too are
soliciting the Most High in line with your prayers, to restore
and maintain his Majesty in good health, as we so devoutly
desire because of the love we bear him.—From Rome, the
day June 11, 1483, in the twelfth year of our Pontificate."*

The text of the second brief with its threat of excommunication is not in the *Liber Brevium.* The Pope evidently had second thoughts and had it destroyed, or no
copies were made. Sixtus, from his personal experience
with the single-minded Calabrian Saint, knew that no one
could influence him and that no one could intimidate him.
Copies of the letter to King Louis and copies of the original briefs were evidently destroyed centuries ago.

Though Louis did not dare confront the Saint with the
threatening second brief and because he was convinced
that none of the plotters against his throne could bribe or
influence him, he decided to try another tack to get the
Saint to cure him. He planned to tempt him in various and
presumably subtle ways. It was common gossip in the
court that the Saint and his friars lived a very austere life,
avoiding social contacts and living on a strict diet of herbs
and fruit. The wily Monarch (according to the testimony

of Jean Thonart, a servant of the King at Tours) with great secrecy ordered Pierre Briconnet and others to keep the four hermits under surveillance at all times, particularly when they were in their room. The King's orders were followed very carefully, for all knew what terrible punishment would be visited on them if the King found out that they were not fulfilling their assignments.

All that they could report to the King, at the regular intervals he required, was that Francis, when in his room, spent his time either kneeling in prayer, his arms extended to God, and his eyes toward Heaven, or sitting on his rough bench lost in deep meditation, or standing up unmoving, contemplating the crucifix on the wall. As these reports continued to come to the suspicious King, he, a highly intelligent man, sometimes became deeply moved, according to observers, clasping his hands in humble thanks that his suspicions were apparently unfounded.

However, this sick King was still not entirely convinced, recalling that during his illness he had been duped by other supposedly holy men. He decided to try other approaches to test the Calabrian, who, despite his worldwide reputation as a miracle worker and healer of the sick, seemed to lack either the power or the desire to heal him. The King listened to the malicious whisperings of cynical courtiers and advisers, who were convinced that the Calabrian Saint was an imposter taking advantage of his generosity and attention. They suggested that the King tempt him with special dishes, so Louis ordered that a basket of freshly caught fish be brought to the Hermit's quarters, telling Francis that they were from the King and that they would be cooked in whatever fashion he wanted them. If Francis did not want them himself, he could turn them over to his three friars. But the Saint sent them back to the King with his and his friars' deepest thanks. This was repeated for several days. Each time Francis would, with great patience, repeat his thanks and send them back. According to the King's counselors, repeated presentation of such delicious morsels would ultimately break down the resistance of the Saint and his three friars. The courtiers, who indulged themselves constantly in luxury and high living, could not understand men of such iron will and extreme self-denial. However, much to their embarrassment, which only increased their hatred of the Calabrian, they were finally, though reluctantly, convinced that the four Calabrian hermits were thoroughly committed to their vows and that nothing would shake them.

The King, now fully convinced that he could not break the friars' resolve through food, decided to try a different method. To demonstrate the high esteem in which he presumably held the Holy Man of Calabria, he next sent him a highly ornate table and a gold and silver service, with an earnest prayer that Francis keep these small gifts as a favor to the King. Just as soon as the Saint saw the table and costly table and kitchen ware, he politely thanked the servants and told them: "Tell his Majesty that these costly utensils are useless to poor hermits, such as myself and my friars. For us a dish, a wooden cup and spoon, and a clay pot are more than sufficient for our needs. Please bring them back to the King with our deepest thanks and the blessing of God."

But the King, under pressure from his advisors, tried another stratagem. He had a set of kitchen utensils made of metal with beautiful designs on them. Again Francis sent them back, telling the bearers again to thank the persistent Louis, but that they had all the cooking utensils they needed. Louis was still determined to break through the Saint's adamant dedication to his most austere and simple existence. One of his counselors suggested that a highly artistic and expensive religious object be made and presented to the Saint. Louis selected a miniature statue of the Holy Virgin Mary, cast in the finest gold and exquisitely fashioned. He sent it to the Saint via one of his most astute counselors with instructions to brush aside all possible arguments and to force Francis to accept the statue as an object of inspiration and devotion. But the Calabrian flatly refused to accept it, telling the bearer:

"Thank the King for his generous gift, and tell him that my devotion is not to gold or silver, but for the Virgin Mother of God, who reigns in Heaven with her divine Son. I have with me an image of the Virgin on paper, and this is sufficient for my needs."

The King refused to accept this rejection as sincere. He sent the statue back twice, each time with one of the most eloquent officers of his court, suggesting to the Saint that if he did not want to keep it for himself and his friars, he could sell it and use the money for the poor. Francis refused, pointing out to the King's representative: "It is not necessary that I get involved in such a matter. The King has his charity workers who are far more competent in disposing of such an object than I."

The golden statue of the Virgin, which was valued at 17,000 ducats, was later donated to the clergy of the Plessis church, who accepted it readily and with great pleasure.

In spite of the persistent refusals, all so different from the attitude of the people in his court, the sick King had still some doubts. Jacques Coittier, his principal physician and the man who had the greatest influence over him and who had suggested some of the methods for tempting the Saint, suggested still another one. Coittier greatly resented the presence of the Calabrian Holy Man, more than anyone else in the court, for the Saint had greatly diminished his control over the dying King, and he wanted to do what he could to discredit him. He suggested that the King, on his next daily visit to the Saint, offer him a purse full of money. The King agreed, and the next time he visited Francis, kneeling before him, he pulled the purse from under his mantle and offered it, saying: "Good Man, now that we are hidden from all eyes, accept this money. It will help you establish a monastery of your order in Rome." The Saint recoiled, obviously deeply offended, and told the King bluntly: "Majesty, instead of giving it to me, why do you not return this money to your subjects, from whom you have so unjustly taken it."

Shocked by this stinging rebuke, and in a consternation that he had never felt before, he hurriedly excused himself. Like King Ferrante of Naples, the proud King of France had to learn the hard way that Francis was truly a saint, completely disdainful of the things of the world—a man who lived solely by his faith in God and his love for his neighbor. With this final attempt to corrupt the Saint a signal failure, one that resulted in the most devastating rebuke the King had ever suffered, Louis became totally convinced of the Saint's holiness and sincerity. The Saint's adamant stand had finally triumphed over the insidious talk and malicious actions of those who hated him. Louis and the royal family accepted Francis for the Saint that he was and showed complete trust in him and his mission. All the King's counselors and courtiers, including the King's top physician, Coittier, knowing the King, treated the Saint with the greatest respect, deferring to him and his friars on all occasions.

There was another memorable shock in store for the King and his family. Early in his stay, while wandering through the woods that surrounded the King's castle, the Calabrian discovered a small cave in a remote area. Occasionally, he would visit this secluded cave and spend several hours in prayer and contemplation. This went on for many months without anyone in the court being aware of it. In fact, his three companion friars also did not know where the Saint sometimes disappeared to for long periods at a time.

Shortly after Louis finally became convinced of the Calabrian's unquestionable saintliness, Princess Anne, Louis' firstborn, was strolling through the forest with several courtiers and ladies-in-waiting. They saw a great glowing light among the trees. When they approached, they saw the Saint at the mouth of the cave in deep contemplation, floating in mid-air, suffused in light. The Princess sent one of the courtiers to summon the King, who hurried to the spot. He watched the glowing Saint in stunned silence, then quietly ordered everyone to leave and to never again approach the area. However, he would from time to time sneak into the woods and watch the Saint in his great moments of divine ecstasy and contemplation. The once cynical tyrant finally understood what the Saint was trying to tell him—that he had to concern himself with his soul rather than his body. This realization brought him a firmer faith and inner peace.

Chapter 19

A KING DIES
A CHRISTIAN DEATH

Finally convinced of the Saint's sincerity and complete commitment to God, Louis resigned himself to the fact that it was not in the power of the Holy Man from Calabria to save him. Resolved to die the good Christian that Francis wanted him to be, he would spend some time each day with the Saint in his cell, where both would pray fervently, the King patiently listening to the Saint's admonitions.

At times when the King was too weak to go to Francis' cell, Francis would visit him in his chambers. The King even adopted the Calabrian's *"Ave Maria"* in greeting his counselors and courtiers. The French ruler, having resigned himself to his fate, became not only more religious but also more cheerful and tolerant of others. This radical change in the once arrogant King made his courtiers happier, once it was determined to be genuine and not just a pretence. All members of the court, including those who still regarded the Saint with ill-disguised contempt, treated the Calabrian with keen respect.

Francis became the King's major confidant, Louis turning to him for advice on affairs of state as well as of religion. The Saint was careful to refer those routine matters to members of the court, who were more understanding and expert. However, he did advise the dying King on some such affairs since he was sometimes able with his prophetic powers to anticipate developments. One matter about which he convinced the French Monarch was restoring the regions of Valentinois and Die to the Holy See. The capital city of this area is Valence, on the east bank of the Rhone, half-way between Avignon and Lyons. This province, long a Papal fief, was ceded by the Holy See to Louis' father, Charles VII. It was created a dukedom for Caesar Borgia, who acquired the title of Duke of Valentinois. Sixtus, sending the Saint a letter of thanks for this restoration, designated Girolamo Riario, his nephew, as ruler, with the title of count. However, shortly after his death this act of Louis was rescinded by his successor.

In the meantime, the Pope's problems in Italy were mounting. The Holy See ended its alliance with the Republic of Venice, the Venetians flatly refusing to raise the siege of Ferrara as the Pope had requested. On May 24, 1483, with the endorsement of the College of Cardinals, the Pope issued an interdict against the Doge and his council, which was distributed to all the Christian reigning heads of state. The Venetians were angered by the Papal bull, fearful of what effect it would have on their commercial operations. Venice was at that time the leading trading nation of Europe and was anxious to keep the goodwill of its European neighbors and safeguard its markets. The Venetians asked that a plenary council be convoked to consider the Papal bull, but their appeal fell on deaf ears. The Emperor of the Holy Roman Empire, the King of England, and Louis of France had the Papal bull reproduced and distributed throughout their kingdoms. Most of the lesser Christian rulers did the same. Francis, as the Vatican's unofficial representative to the court of France, of course urged King Louis to publish the bull, to send the Venetian ambassador back to Venice, and to ask other European rulers to follow suit.

Documents in the Vatican Archives indicate that the Pope had sent secret instructions to the Calabrian Saint through his emissary at the court of France, Andrea di Grimaldi, to see that the King of France would speedily carry out the Pope's request, setting an example for the other reigning monarchs. After the bull had been distributed, Sixtus wrote to Francis asking him to thank the King for the effective way in which he had fulfilled the Pope's request.

During this international crisis, the King's health deteriorated steadily. He grew constantly weaker and more dependent on the Calabrian Man of God for consolation and support, much to the annoyance of the counselors and ministers of the French court. However, they showed at all times proper deference to the Saint. Francis had become indispensable to the moribund King, for only his words and prayers comforted him and brought him the inner peace he needed. The Saint had convinced him that no matter what he could do, there was no hope for him—the Creator had willed his death.

However, the King kept hoping against hope that somehow the Saint might be able to cure him. One day toward the end of August, 1483 (as reported by the royal chaplain who was present), the King said to Francis: "Good Man, from you I expect a precise answer on three questions which are disturbing me deeply, and you can make me happy because I know that the Lord has given you special power that lights the future. You are to tell me once and for all whether I shall ever be cured, how I shall treat the demands of the King of Aragon for the regions of Rousillon and Cerdan, and what calamity will visit France after my death."

The Saint replied: "Sire, no one on earth can presume to alter the divine will. It is our duty to submit ourselves humbly and prayerfully to this will. When I was first called by you, I refused to come because I did not want to leave the area of my holy mission; but when I finally understood it to be the will of God that I should come to you, I did not hesitate, aware that I alone could make you understand God's holy will. Therefore, O King, I must inform you with deep regret that God will not permit me to cure you. You must put your affairs in order, because little time remains for you. In regard to your differences with the King of Aragon, grant him what he asks. To your third query, I can only answer with grave concern. After your passing, France will be devastated by a great heresy."

Having resigned himself to his death as the will of God a

month or so before this conversation, the King shrugged his shoulders helplessly. Regarding the dispute with the King of Spain, in his will he instructed his successor to cede Rousillon and Cerdan—the territory on the eastern end of the Pyrenees—to Spain, which his successor, Charles VIII, finally did. As to the prediction of heresy in France, the King, though deeply moved, saw it as beyond his scope. After this request, the King made no further demands on the Calabrian, gratefully sharing many hours of prayer and meditation with him. He concentrated on getting his kingdom in order and arranging for his son to succeed him. He brought the Dauphin to Plessis, where he instructed the Prince on what he should do to be a better king than he had been. He advised him to be less severe with the nobles and members of the royal family than he had been, and to reduce taxes and tolls, which he had raised so many times during his reign and which were a burden to his subjects. These admonitions to the Dauphin were obviously the result of Francis' blunt talks with the King regarding the oppression of his subjects and treatment of his officers. The King also insisted that the reduction in taxes and tolls should be made law by the National Assembly and the Chamber of Counts. He then called all members of the royal family together and designated the Dauphin as King, with his oldest daughter, Anne, as Regent until he would reach his majority, and he turned over the seals of state to them. Louis requested his children to be faithful to each other and to their subjects, particularly to "The Good Man," Francis of Paola. He asked them to seek his counsel and his prayers.

Freed from cares of state, Louis, aware of his imminent death, concerned himself with the salvation of his soul. Obviously wracked with mounting pain, he suffered in silence, asking only that "The Good Man" stay at his side to comfort and console him.

A few days later, on Monday, August 25, he suffered a severe stroke, that robbed him temporarily of his physical senses and of his speech. However, he soon regained consciousness of his surroundings. The royal physician, Coittier, after examining him, stated that he did not believe the King would survive the night. When this information was conveyed to the Calabrian Saint in his cell, Francis hurried to the King and informed him that he would survive through the coming Saturday, five days away. This raised the spirits of the dying Monarch, since Saturday is the day devoted to the Virgin Mary, to whom he had become particularly attached. Having regained his faculties, he confessed himself with deep reverence, received the Sacraments, and calm and resigned, he lay back on his pillows, repeating: "Our Lady of Embrun, dear Mother, help me."

Saturday, August 30, 1483, at eight o'clock in the evening, the prediction of the Calabrian Holy Man came true. The King of France, the most powerful monarch of his day, at age seventy-one, died the death of a good Christian, which he had not been during the height of his power. This amazing change was the result of four months of diligent work and prayer by the Saint from Paola. His biographer, de Commines, was able to write: "I have never seen any man die so peacefully." The King was buried with the traditional pomp by pall bearers he had personally designated. Francis did not attend the funeral. He locked himself in his cell for several days to pray for the departed King.

At the family gathering Louis had established his fourteen-year-old son, Charles, as his successor and, wise in the ways of politics, designated his eldest daughter, Anne, the wife of Peter of Bourbon, Lord of the Beaujolais region, as regent until Charles reached his twenty-first year, in 1493. Anne, despite the opposition of the powerful Duke of Orleans, won the endorsement of the heads of the various French states gathered at Tours. Once confirmed, Anne selected ten of the realm's wisest leaders as her Royal Council. She became in effect, though not in name, the Queen of France. A shrewd administrator, Anne dismissed dishonest officials who had enjoyed the favor of her dying father, including the court physician, Coittier. As already indicated, she had the highest regard for Francis and ordered that he and his friars should have the respect of all courtiers. Following King Louis' burial, the Paolan Saint retired to the solitude of his cell. He did not approve of some of Anne's actions but felt that they were beyond his concern.

During the regency of Anne, Francis had only two friars with him, his nephew, Brother Nicola d'Alessio, and Father Bernardino di Cropalati. Because of an infraction of the Saint's rules, Father Giovanni Cadurio had been sent back to Calabria, to the monastery of the Holy Trinity at Spezzano Grande. Francis approached the Cardinal of Tours, Elia de Bourdeille, A Franciscan and a great admirer and friend of the Calabrian, for help in establishing a monastery of his order at Plessis. The Cardinal was pleased with the proposal and agreed to prevail on Anne, the Regent, to approve the Saint's request. Anne was pleased with the idea and signed the necessary orders. Unfortunately, before the monastery was completed, the Cardinal died, and he was denied the opportunity to bless the first community of the Minimi in France, much to Francis' regret.

Once the monastery was completed, many candidates presented themselves to be novices under the Saint's strict rules. After interviewing all the candidates, the Saint selected twelve, as Christ had done with His Apostles. One of the first accepted was Father Germain Lionnet, a native of Tours. He later was sent as a missionary to Spain, where he had great success and founded several monasteries of the Congregation. In 1511 he was elected the third head of the Order. He died two years later.

Chapter 20

THE LOVE AND RESPECT
OF THE REGENT

With the death of King Louis, who had been so generous and devoted to him, Francis became concerned with legalizing his ownership of the residence (near the entrance to the castle) that had been given him by the dead King. The house had been donated to him officially by the King in the presence of several counselors and courtiers, who could vouch for the fact. However, the Saint was disturbed that he did not have official documents definitely deeding the structure to his order, since this might prove an embarrassment in the future.

He mentioned this fact to Princess Anne, asking that his Order's title to the property be made a matter of written record. The Regent, who was not a religious woman, but had the deepest respect and regard for the Calabrian Saint, readily approved the request, and ordered her legal counselor to prepare the necessary documents. However, because of the political turmoil and intrigue prevalent in France, it was more than a year after the Regent's approval that the title papers were drafted. They were signed and sealed on March 19, 1485. The royal decree read:

"We remember well how our Lord and father prevailed on the said Francis of Paola to come to him, and as an indication of the great love and sincere affection he had for him, donated to him and his friars the said chapel of Iselle and its contents, to hold and use as they saw fit; and as is apparent since the death of our Lord and father, the chapel has been used for honest purposes and ends, including daily prayers

*for our Lord and father and for ourselves; to carry on such
and related duties with greater ease and freedom, we order
the Governor of Turaine to see that the said Francis of Paola
and his friars shall in no way every be molested in their free
use of the chapel, its contents and other effects assigned to
them by our Lord and father."*

In the meantime, the Saint continued his campaign to
have his Congregation receive full canonical approval
from the Holy See. One year after the death of Louis XI,
Pope Sixtus IV died, on August 29, 1484. He was succeeded by Cardinal Giambattista Cibo of Genoa, as Innocent VIII. Francis urged the new Pope to give full approval to all the rules of his Congregation of Hermit
Friars. His request was accompanied by a recommendation from Charles VIII. On March 21, 1485, Innocent
VIII issued a decree, *"Pastoris Officium,"* granting blanket
apostolic approval to all privileges and rights requested by
the Calabrian organizer.

Having received this blanket approval from the reigning
Pontiff, Francis proceeded to have his order recognized
officially and legally by the ecclesiastical and civil authorities throughout France. In this regard, he asked the
Regent for permission to publish and distribute everywhere in France the rules, privileges and rights confirmed
apostolically by the Pope. As expected, the Regent readily
approved the Saint's request. Because of the bureaucratic
procedure that existed, more than three years elapsed before the Regent's orders were fulfilled on April 18, 1488.
The royal letter read:

*"The King, in response to the request of our dear and most
loving Brother Francis of Paola, grants to him and his present and future friars, the faculty and right to publish as they
see fit, the Papal letter, and to enjoy all the privileges and
rights contained therein, according to their form and
tenor . . . We pray all archbishops, bishops and other ecclesiastical dignitaries, to receive the Hermit Friars and their suc-*

cessors, and to permit them to establish locations for their oratories and monasteries, which they will be offered presently or in years to come for their divine purposes. The King further declares that these friars are under his sovereign protection, so that they can with zeal and with peace serve God, our Creator."

As a result of this royal decree, many came to the castle at Plessis, seeking entry into the Congregation of the Hermit Friars. It soon became evident that the quarters allowed them at Plessis were far too small to accommodate them. Princess Anne and the young King realized that larger and more private quarters would have to be provided.

On April 24, 1489, a royal decree was issued stating that His Majesty had decided to construct for the Friars in a more isolated area of the Parc another church and monastery, furnished with many dormitories, a cloister, a garden and all other exigencies required for monastic life. There being no place within the Plessis-du-Parc, it was decided to build the church just aside of the Parc area on the banks of the Cher, a stream that empties into the River Loire. The area was known as the Montils. Part of the land to be used belonged to David Lemaitre, who was a witness at the canonization hearing at Tours. Lemaitre stated that the Calabrian Miracle Worker had contacted him and asked him if he felt that the price he was being offered was satisfactory, for, if it were not, the Saint would see that a satisfactory price would be paid.

The King authorized his trusted counselor, Renato Cymier, a wise, competent, conscientious and hard-working man, to supervise the construction work and to pay the bills. He authorized Cymier to sell all the iron gates around the castle at Plessis to obtain funds for the new construction. The young King further ordered his treasurer, Peter Briconnet, to cover all other expenses. The construction work went on throughout the year 1491, Francis watching the progress with keen interest. One day, while he was present, the workers turned up a nest of snakes. They were preparing to burn them out when the Saint intervened, saying: "In the name of Charity, do not hurt these poor creatures. Tomorrow they will no longer be here." After dark, Francis went to the spot, picked up the snakes in his hands and carried them up the bank of the Cher, far away from the construction site.

According to the desire of the Calabrian, the new monastery was a two-story building, with a conference room, a dispensary, a kitchen and eating area, fourteen regular cells, two prison cells (for delinquents), and a sanctuary, which opened into the church. The building cost the King more than 7,400 lire, a large sum in those days.

Francis moved to the new buildings sometime before they were finished and was joined by his seven brother friars as soon as quarters were ready for them. He also transferred all the furnishings from the old quarters and chapel. The King arranged for the community to receive 500 lire tornese each year for the maintenance and care of the new community. In subsequent centuries, the monastery was enlarged and decorated with beautiful religious paintings. Francis' cell was in a special location, removed from the cells of his friars and adjacent to the church and the wall facing Plessis, so that he could be available to those who sought him without interfering with the other friars. In the solitude of this special cell, the Saint passed the last sixteen years of his life. Here the young King would visit him regularly. After Francis' death, his cell was transformed into a chapel at the expense of Jacqueline Maulandrin, the widow of his nephew, Andrea d'Alessio, who had moved from Calabria to Tours. It soon became one of the most venerated sanctuaries in France, where prelates came to say Mass and where a constant stream of faithful came to pray to the Saint for favors. In 1561, the body of his nephew was transferred to the site.

The church was built after the monastery had been finished. The church was designed by Pierre Machy, the leading architect of Tours. It was twenty-five meters in length,

ten meters wide and twelve meters in height. The church
was beautified by works of Michael Tholeppe, a brilliant
sculptor. Stained windows, painted by Gilles Jourdain, a
master craftsman, represented pious events. Francis dedicated this first church of his order in France to Jesus and
Mary, and the two chapels that adjoined it were dedicated
to the Blessed Virgin and St. John the Baptist.

All of these favors conferred on the Calabrian Servant
of God, though carrying the authorization of the young
King, were actually the work of Princess Anne, the Regent, who at that time was in complete control of the government. This Princess, in spite of her worldly interest,
held the Good Hermit in high esteem and reverence. And
Francis rewarded her by predicting something that she had
thought she would never know. Anne was deeply involved
in the affairs of state and had few occasions to visit with
the Calabrian Holy Man. One day she came to him very
sad and dispirited. She confided in him that though she
had been married many years, she had never had a child,
and she told him she so wanted to be a mother. The Saint
told her: "Madam, do not concern yourself unduly. Before
I leave France, you shall have the heir you so desire." A
year later, Princess Anne had her first child, Charles of
Bourbon, Count of Clermont. Sometime later, the Saint, in
writing to the Princess, told her that she would have another child. His most trusted friar, who later wrote his first
biography, felt that such a prediction was dangerous.
Francis reproved him, telling him: "Let us allow God to
do His will." Several months later, the Regent had a second child, a daughter, who was baptized Suzanne, and became the wife of the Duke of Montpensier.

In gratitude, Princess Anne built a new monastery for
the Saint, near the city of Gien, on the Loire, on the other
side of Orleans. The new monastery, a magnificent building, was dedicated to the Holy Trinity and St. Helena. The
construction began in 1493, but it was not finished until
1498. Father Bernardo Otranto was appointed superior or
"corrector" (the title preferred by Francis) of this second

monastery in France. In 1562 the Gien monastery was devastated by Huguenot vandals. However, it was fully restored by Peter Fortet, a Protestant nobleman, who had participated in the attack and had repented his sacrilegious action and had returned to the Church.

Princess Anne, who became Duchess of Bourbon and d'Auvergne, after her brother reached his majority and became King, outlived Francis by fifteen years, dying in 1522. In 1516, on May 1, she wrote to Pope Leo X, urging the canonization of the Calabrian Holy Man. When the canonization occurred, she participated in the solemn celebration in France that followed.

Chapter 21

AN AMBITIOUS KING
SEES THE LIGHT

In 1491, when Charles VIII reached his majority, he assumed the throne and married Anne, duchess of Brittany. Though he abandoned the wise and progressive policies carried out by his sister Anne during her Regency, he maintained a deep regard and devotion for the Calabrian Holy Man.

The young Monarch continued frequent visits to the Saint's cell and spent many hours with him. Often he would ask Francis to visit with him at his palace at Amboise. While he was with the Calabrian, he always kept his head uncovered, as an indication of the respect he had for him.

Father Stephen Joly, one of the friars at the Montils monastery close to Francis and one of the fifty-seven witnesses at the canonization hearing at Tours in 1513, related an incident involving the young King. One day the young Monarch, while still living in the palace at Plessis, sought to visit the Saint in his cell to discuss a problem he had. Father Peter Gilbert, the superior, went to the cell and knocked, repeating the ejaculation, *"Ave Maria,"* as required. He said: "Father, the King is here, and he wishes to speak with you." Receiving no reply, the superior knocked the second time, repeating his words. Still no reply, and a third knock brought the same results. For eight days the Saint remained locked in his cell, not seeing anyone.

The superior, deeply disturbed, told the King that he was not able to get a response from the Saint. Charles then went to the cell himself and knocked, using the standard greeting, *"Ave Maria."* "Father, I would like to speak with you," he said in a loud voice. On receiving no reply, the King became alarmed. Afraid that something serious had happened to the Calabrian Hermit, he ordered the door broken in. Just as the friars were ready to do so, they heard a cough, indicating that the Saint was alive and well, but so involved in his meditation that he did not want to be disturbed. The King understood and, respecting the Saint's wishes, quietly withdrew.

During the civil war in Burgundy between the King and his cousin Louis, Duke of Orleans (who was allied with the Duke of Burgundy), the Saint, fully aware of the importance of victory for the young Monarch, spent all together twenty-two days in deep prayer and meditation for his success. On the twenty-third day he issued from his cell and in a relieved voice informed his friars that the King had won a great victory at Saint Aubin, ending the bloody civil war. Francis motioned to his friars to kneel and led them in prayers of thanksgiving. The next day, when the news of the King's victory reached Plessis, there was a great celebration in the castle.

Gregorio di Vico, a Neapolitan officer serving Charles, had received a blessed candle from Francis, which he still had with him during the Battle of St. Aubin, where he was struck on the brow by shrapnel. This normally would have killed him, but it left him with only a few scratches. When di Vico returned to Plessis, he sought out the Saint, to thank him for the miraculous way his life had been spared and asked to be received into his Congregation. He was readily accepted, and in 1513, when Father Martin la Haye made a report on the monastery, he indicated that di Vico was still at Plesis and was a devout and fervent member of the Order.

To avoid further bloodshed between warring factions in France, the Saint had, during private talks with Charles, promoted marriage with Duchess Anne of Brittany. However, the Saint's proposal faced some obstacles, including

the necessity of obtaining a special dispensation from the
Pope because Charles and Anne were related by blood.
Besides, Anne had been betrothed to Maximilian I, the
King of Austria, and Charles had been more or less betrothed to Marguerite of Bourgogne. The Saint, through
his prophetic powers, was aware that to save France from
more bloody civil wars, these two had to marry. On December 6, 1491 the two were wed. Immediately after the
marriage, the King and his bride visited the Saint at the
cloister at Plessis and expressed their gratitude and asked
for his blessing. The marriage achieved the political unity
of France that Louis XI had so long desired.

Concerning these events Father Bourdalue wrote as follows:

*"France is indebted to Francis of Paola for the success it
achieved at that time and enjoys now by being united with
Brittany. It is to the Saint from Paola that our kings are in
debt, for acquisition of this rich and powerful territory, the
most fruitful of French provinces. Brittany is in debt also to
the Saint for having been placed under the rule of the most
Christian monarchs of the age."*

Queen Anne, on her first meeting with him at Plessis-du-
Parc, became devoted to the Calabrian Holy Man and
held him in deep reverence and esteem. To show this admiration, the King and Queen had the Dauphin baptized
by the Holy Man in their royal chapel. It was October 13,
1492, one day after Columbus had discovered America.
The child was christened Charles Roland, in memory of
his celebrated forbear, Charlemagne, and Charlemagne's
famous knight.

The Queen was a most devout follower of Francis and
frequently sought his company. She had supreme faith in
him. Once when she became seriously ill and her doctors
feared for her recovery, she asked for help from the Saint.
He sent her three apples with instruction to eat them. Her
physicians forbade her to eat them, telling her that they

would greatly worsen her condition. She refused to listen to them. Convinced that the Saint's gifts, along with his prayers, would help her, she ate them. No sooner had she finished than she was freed of her illness.

On another occasion, with the King present, the Holy Man told her that God would make her the mother of three children, two sons and a daughter. He added that the children would grow and prosper as long as the parents practiced their faith truly and obeyed the divine laws. If they did not, he warned them, God would take the children away. The terrible prediction became a reality when Charles ignored the Saint's admonitions and pursued his worldly conquests. Charles Roland, the first-born, died one year after he had been baptized; a second son lived only twenty-three days; and the daughter lived only one year.

Though the King continued to show the greatest respect for the Calabrian Holy Man, he continued also to ignore his admonitions. He listened to the counsel of ambitious and flattering courtiers such as the Count Dunois, who appealed to his hunger for power and glory. Foremost among his ambitions was reconquering the Kingdom of Naples, once the possession of the House of Anjou. Ferrante, King of Naples, died in January, 1494, at age seventy-one. He was succeeded by his son, Alfonso II.

Determined to reclaim the Italian lands ruled by his ancestors, Charles VIII made concessions to Ferdinand and Isabella of Spain and to Maximilian of Austria in order to keep them neutral. Then, on September 3, 1494, he crossed the Alps into Italy with an army of 50,000, meeting little or no resistance, and marched down to Rome. The reigning Pope, Alexander VI, had already recognized Alfonso II as the rightful King of Naples. Unable to prevail on the Pope to withdraw this approval, the young King sought an alliance with Ludwig the Moor of Milan, and neutrality from Venice. The Calabrian Saint, of course, had done what he could to dissuade the headstrong French King from carrying out this dangerous enterprise, but his advice fell on deaf ears. Charles had to learn the will of God the hard way.

Ignoring the Pope and his Italian allies, Charles marched to Naples. With Alfonso retreating to the Island of Ischia, he entered Naples on February 22 and was greeted as a liberator by the enthusiastic populace. However, when he learned that the Northern Italian states had allied against him, Charles decided to give up his claim and return to France. At Fornovo, a small town near Parma, in Reggio Emilia, the French King was confronted by the Italian Confederation. The date was July 6, 1495. The Marquis Francis Gonzaga, of Mantua, was commander-in-chief of the Italian forces. After a bitter and bloody battle, Charles was able to fight through the Italian forces, reaching Asti in the Piedmont region. From there he bargained with Ludwig Sforza, of Milan, to lift the siege of Ravenna, in which his cousin, the Duke of Orleans, had been trapped. Thanks to the prayers of the Calabrian Holy Man, Charles came safely through his Italian misadventure. Though he toyed for several months with the idea of another attempt to regain control of Naples, when he learned that the Spaniards under the great general Gonsalvo de Cordova had reinforced the Neapolitan armies, he abandoned it. The Italian fiasco made him pay more attention to the admonitions of the Saint. He resumed his visits to Francis in his cell at Montils and, on occasions, would arrange to have him brought to his palace at Amboise.

Under the influence of the Calabrian Saint, Charles became much more thoughtful and contented, as well as more concerned with his religion. He made wiser decisions and initiated many needed political reforms, taking as a model his ancestor, St. Louis (King of France from 1226 to 1270), who had ruled the country with great wisdom and saintliness.

Meditating on the life of his ancestor—the King who became a saint—and helped by the Calabrian, Charles gradually became more and more committed to his religion. On one occasion he confided to his sister, Jeanne, a devout Catholic, that he had resolved never to commit mortal sin again. At that time he was twenty-eight years of age, and had, thanks to the presence of the Holy Man from Calabria, completely changed his way of life, his counselors, and his ambitions.

On April 7, 1498, after dinner, he and his wife, Queen Anne, decided to watch a basketball game in the courtyard of the castle at Amboise. They were making their way through a gallery that was about to be demolished when they came to a door that was broken down. Charles, in the darkness, struck his head violently against the broken upper frame of the door and fell backwards unconscious. Twice he regained consciousness, dazedly calling on God, the Virgin, St. Claude, and St. Blaise to come to his aid. But a few hours later, with the bishop of Angers at his bedside, he expired.

The ominous prediction of the Hermit Saint to Louis XI had been fulfilled. Charles left no heirs and the Valois line died with him. But the Saint's own work was greatly advanced; both Regent Anne and Charles had encouraged and helped the Saint to establish monasteries throughout France, aided by the bishops and members of the nobility.

In 1490 Francis supervised the building of the monastery of the Blessed Virgin and All Saints at Amboise, where Charles, then twelve, first met and paid homage to him. In 1491, the monastery of Our Lady of Mercy was constructed in Frejus, which he had freed of a devastating plague when he first landed in France in 1483. In 1492, the first monastery in Spain was built, St. Mary of Victory, at Malaga, on the southern Mediterranean coast of the peninsula. The Moors just that year had surrendered this Spanish port to Ferdinand and Isabella, the patrons of Christopher Columbus. A few weeks before the surrender, possibly through heavenly intercession, the Saint had dispatched two of his most devoted priests, Fathers Bernardino di Cropalati and Jaime Lespervier, to advise the Spanish monarchs to continue the siege, that God would grant them victory. A short time later, the Moors' re-sistance collapsed, and Ferdinand and Isabella entered Malaga in triumph. Shortly after the victory, the Spanish rulers had an oratory built on the very spot where they had pitched their royal tent during the siege and sent a message of thanks to the Saint. The liberated people of Malaga called the Minimi "Friars of Victory."

Chapter 22

A WORLDLY KING
AND A SAINTLY QUEEN

With the tragic, untimely death of Charles VIII in 1498, the Calabrian Holy Man, now eighty-two years of age and having completed sixteen years in France, felt that his mission in that country had been fulfilled and that he should return to his beloved Calabria.

Louis XII, Duke of Orleans, whose grandfather was Gian Galeazzo Visconti, Count of Milan, succeeded to the French throne. He was a distant cousin of Charles VIII through his great grandfather, Charles V, and being born in 1462, was eight years older than Charles. He established his court at his castle near Blois, some fifty miles northeast of Tours, on the River Loire.

The new French King may have seen the great Miracle Worker on some of his infrequent visits to the royal court, but when he became King, he did not know too much about him. His branch of the Valois house was not very welcome at the court of Louis XI or of Charles VIII, and when he reached his majority as Duke of Orleans, he was involved in a number of plots against his ruling cousins.

With Louis XII's accession to the throne, the Saint sent Father Binet, his most trusted assistant, and another friar to the new King at Blois to request a safe conduct order through France so that he could return to his native Calabria. Louis, who knew of Francis in very general terms, readily acceded to the Saint's request. However, as soon as George Cardinal Amboise, the Archbishop of Rouen, heard of the King's action, he strongly implored him to withdraw the permission, pointing out the wonderful things the Saint had accomplished for his predecessors and for the people of France. Other dignitaries of the Church and members of the nobility added their plea to that of the Cardinal.

When Father Binet returned to the monastery with the King's safe conduct order, Francis, with a couple of his Calabrian friars as companions, immediately began his long trip back to his native land. He was already on his way toward Lyons when the King's messenger reached him with the King's order countermanding his approval of the Saint's departure and requesting his return to the Montils monastery. A few days later, the new King came to Plessis and the monastery at Montils. There he spent three hours in private conversation with the Saint in his cell. When the Monarch came out he was very solemn and deeply moved. With tears in his eyes he said to those who had accompanied him: "I would have never believed that there was a man so holy on earth. I swear to you that he revealed to me secrets hidden in my mind that only God could know."

Obviously one of the secrets that the Saint had revealed was the King's intention to gain an annulment of his marriage with Jeanne of Valois, the deformed younger daughter of King Louis XI. The Calabrian Holy Man had the deepest concern for the unfortunate Queen, whom he had known as a child. She was a kind, humble person with a physical defect, who had been forced into a marriage of convenience by her father. A pious person, she was repelled by the ephemeral gaiety and pomp of the royal court. She preferred the simple quiet life of the castle of Linieres. She was forced by her father, Louis XI, for political reasons, to marry Louis of Orleans, whom she greatly feared. When her husband neglected her, his angry father-in-law publicly threatened to throw him into the sea.

In his three-hour meeting with the new King of France, Francis convinced him that he should permit Jeanne to follow the life of piety and contemplation she wanted, while he pursued his worldly ambitions and interests. The fact that her husband had hated her father and was involved in plots against him grieved Jeanne greatly and made her seek the Saint's comfort. After his defeat by his cousin, Charles VIII, at the battle of Saint Aubin, the Duke was imprisoned for two years. Jeanne, as a dutiful wife, visited him daily and saw to it that he received proper care. However, the Duke found no happiness in the devotion and concern of his physically unattractive wife. Nevertheless, she pleaded with her brother, Charles VIII, to forgive her rebellious husband and release him.

Strangely enough, when he finally gained the throne, Louis proved himself generous toward his enemies, treating them with great kindness. He remains famous for the statement: "A King of France does not remember the injuries done to the Duke of Orleans." This declaration is an indication of the Christianizing influence of the Calabrian Holy Man on one who theretofore had had little respect for his fellow countrymen or their rights.

Unfortunately, the Monarch's generosity did not extend to his devoted and pious spouse. Shortly after he succeeded to the throne, he petitioned the Pope for dissolution of the marriage. In his petition he claimed that he had been forced by Louis XI, against his will, to marry Jeanne and that the marriage had never been consummated.

On July 29, 1498, the Pope appointed a commission of top prelates, who, after examination of the facts, recommended to the Pontiff, on December 7, that the marriage be annulled. During the three months of the Papal commission's investigation, Queen Jeanne was constantly being consoled by the Calabrian Friar at the monastery of Montils or at the one in Amboise. On being advised of the Papal decision by the Cardinal of Luxembourg, Queen Jeanne exclaimed: "God be blessed! And also he who has broken my chains. From now on I can serve Him better than I did before!" King Louis gave his ex-wife the Duchy of Berry near Bourges, to which she retired on March 12, 1499, and remained for the rest of her life, praying and performing acts of kindness that endeared her to the peo-

ple of Bourges. Here she founded the Franciscan Order of
The Sisters of the Annunciation of Bourges, a dream she
had nurtured from her childhood, when she had developed
a strong devotion to the Blessed Virgin. She was, of
course, encouraged and assisted in realizing this ambition
by the Calabrian Holy Man. Though there appears to have
been an exchange of letters between the Saint and the
Queen, none of these has survived. The Queen, who because of her deformity was always sickly and weak, died
February 4, 1505, in the odor of sanctity. On May 20,
1930, she was canonized as St. Jeanne of Valois by Pope
Pius XI. Her feast day is the day of her death, February 4.

Many Catholics were confused by the Pope's dissolution
of the marriage, but the Calabrian Holy Man, through his
prophetic powers, already knew what the Pope's decision
was to be, accepting it as consistent with the will of God
and in the best interest of the Church and its people. History has confirmed both the soundness and the holiness of
the Pope's action.

As an indication of the divine justification of what had
transpired, Francis participated at the wedding of Louis
XII with the widow of Charles VIII, Anne of Brittany, in
1499, giving it his endorsement. The new Queen, who had
always been popular with the French people, became even
more popular, as Louis XII, for his part, became a most
clement and gentle ruler. He, like his predecessors, treated
the Calabrian Holy Man with great deference and respect
and frequently consulted and prayed with him in the solitude of his cell. However, he would not abandon the
French ambition to gain control of Italy and reclaim the
throne of Naples. He led several armies into Italy and
made numerous alliances with the Italian princes, but was
unable to achieve the success he sought. His various ex-
peditions there resulted in little bloodshed, and credit for
this can be given to the fervent prayers and supplications
of the Calabrian Hermit, whom the King held in such
reverence.

To show his high regard for the Holy Man and for his

congregation, on August 18, 1498, he reconfirmed and added to all the privleges that had been granted by Louis XI and Charles VIII and extended to them complete royal protection. On January 18, 1499, the King broadened these grants by exempting the Hermit Friars from all duties, taxes, and toll fees throughout his kingdom. In these decrees, Louis identified the Calabrian as "our dearest and most beloved brother." The King further decreed that all official documents from the Holy See relating to the Order, as well as those issued by him and his predecessors, be published with the statement that they were being issued by the "founding sovereign, protector and custodian of the said Order, to which, following the example of our predecessors, we demonstrate our profound love and devotion, duly respecting all strict requirements of the rules, and the goodness of our said brother Francis and all his friars."

As a result of King Louis' obviously sincere regard for the Calabrian Saint, Francis was treated with great respect and reverence by all the members of the court and French nobility and by Church dignitaries. However, the Saint was particularly happy over the friendship of two powerful confidants of the King, George Cardinal Amboise, a former minister of King Louis XI, and Simon Robertot, Controller-General of the King's finances. Both constantly pointed out to the King the great service and example that the Calabrian Holy Man and his friars were rendering the King and his subjects. The two wrote many letters to the King on matters relating to the Saint and his activities, of which two have been preserved.

One of these letters was concerned with the erection of a wall around the monastery of Montils, and the other requested special consideration for Francis' nephew, Andrea d'Alessio, the third son of his sister, Brigida, who had joined him at Plessis in 1483 and who, through the intercession of the Saint, had entered the service of the King. In his letter to the Cardinal on behalf of his nephew, Francis pointed out that Andrea was fluent in Italian and French and that he could be utilized at a higher level of work than what he was currently doing.

Though Francis was greatly disappointed on not being able to return to his native Calabria with the passing of Charles VIII, he resigned himself to his fate as being the will of God. He continued to pray for the King and to counsel him on matters concerning which the King requested his advice. A French biographer has stated that there is no doubt the reason King Louis XII was hailed as the "Father of His People" was due primarily to the saintly advice he received from the Calabrian Hermit friar. Under the influence of Francis, the King overcame his reputation as a rebel—gained as a young man—and now enjoyed the respect, trust and love of his subjects and the French nobility and clergy.

In 1500, at the request of the Pope, Louis had marched into Lombardy to prevent Ludwig Sforza, the Moor, from regaining control of Milan. He captured Ludwig and his brother, Ascanio Cardinal Sforza, who had openly used his high office to help his brother. Both brothers were imprisoned in France, Ludwig in the fortress of Loches, in Turenne, and the Cardinal, who had been made prisoner by the Venetians and turned over to the French, in the tower of Bourges. Francis, called to Bourges by the former Queen Jeanne, visited the Cardinal in his prison and assured him that he would soon be released. At the time, this appeared impossible. Pope Alexander VI (1492-1503) had been greatly angered by the Cardinal's actions on behalf of his brothers and had confiscated all the Cardinal's art treasures and distributed all his worldly goods to the poor. However, Francis, who obviously understood Cardinal Sforza's compulsion to help his brother regain freedom for the Milanese, solicited Cardinal Amboise to prevail on the King to release the prelate into the Cardinal's care. On January 3, 1503, Cardinal Sforza was freed and turned over to Cardinal Amboise, who escorted him personally to Rome to make his peace with the Pope. The Pope forgave him, and in 1503 he participated in the election of Alexander's successor, Pius III (Francesco Piccolomini, nephew of Pius II). In May, 1506, he died from the plague, fully reconciled to the Church.

The Calabrian Holy Man, concerned with gaining the broadest possible recognition for his Order, prevailed on King Louis to obtain a new approval for his strict rules from the Pope. The Monarch, always anxious to please his saintly *"Bon Homme,"* obtained through his ambassador at the Vatican this sweeping approval from the new Pope. There is a directive from the King dated January 8, 1502, preserved in the monastery at Tours, instructing all ecclesiastical and civil authorities in France to grant the requests of the Saint and to cooperate with him in every way to advance the Order and its good works.

When Frederick of Aragon, King of Spain, in 1504 forced off the throne of Naples Ferdinand II, son of King Ferrante, Ferdinand asked for asylum from the French King, through the intercession of the Calabrian Saint (whom he had accompanied to France in 1483 at the request of his father). Not only did Louis honor the Saint's request, but he made the deposed Neapolitan monarch the Duke of Anjou, with a large annual income. Ferdinand passed away suddenly on November 9, 1504, a good Christian, thanks to the prayers and saintly admonition of his friend and mentor, Francis of Paola. Ferdinand had insisted that he be buried in the chapel of the Hermit Friars at Montils until his body might be returned to Naples to be buried among his ancestors.

There remain two documents dated November 15, 1504, relating to the disposition of the body of Ferdinand II and his effects. One stated that the body was to rest in the chapel at Montils until such time as it could be transported to Naples and buried. This was signed by the dead King's widow, Isabella, by members of Neapolitan King's court, by Francis of Paola, and by twenty-two of his Hermit Friars and witnessed by several members of the French Court. The second document, also elaborately notarized, contained an inventory of the jewels and precious items buried with the King. Francis assisted with the funeral ceremony, visibly moved, partly for the death of a monarch of whom he was a subject and who had been so helpful to him, and partly because of memories and thoughts of his native land, which was now under foreign rule and which he knew it to be the Will of God he would never see again.

By the age of eighty-eight, the humble Calabrian Miracle Worker, a man clothed always in a simple, threadbare tunic, who lived on the strictest of diets (fruits and vegetables), had not only brought back to life a number of people and worked many other great miracles, but had been a major influence in the lives of five Kings—Ferrante and Ferdinand of Naples plus Louis XI, Charles VIII, and Louis XII of France—and in the pontificates of seven Popes—Pius II, Paul II, Sixtus IV, Innocent VIII, Alexander VI, Pius III, and Julius II. Even his idol and namesake, St. Francis of Assisi, could not boast such a record.

Chapter 23

THE THREE ORDERS

With the sudden death at Tours of Ferdinand II of Naples, and with Louis XII made a kinder and wiser king by his influence, the Calabrian Saint, now nearing his ninetieth year, felt that it was time to turn away from the world of men, and to put in order his spiritual affairs, with which he was primarily concerned.

Despite, or because of, his many years of strict diet, self-denial and self-mortification, he was in full control of his faculties and mentally and spiritually alert. However, weariness was in his bones; he could not get around as he had in the past; and he felt that his God-ordained mission to the lay world had been fulfilled.

The French people were enjoying the rule of a far more humane monarch than they had when he first arrived, and even his beloved Calabria was under the rule of the benign Ferdinand V of Aragon, called "The Catholic," who had chased the Moors out of Spain and backed Columbus' discovery of America. (Ferdinand's famous Queen, Isabella, also known as "The Catholic," a great and pious woman, died in 1504.) Despite the fact that his native land was under a more desirable rule, he was pleased that God had permitted him to be present at the untimely death of Ferrante's son and that he had been instrumental in obtaining asylum for him from Louis XII and was able to counsel him during his last days.

The Calabrian Saint realized that it would not be long before he would be called by Almighty God to join Him among the blessed. With this in mind, he spent more and more time in his cell in prayer, meditation, and ecstasy, during which he would be transported out of his worldly environment, clothed in glowing light and floating in mid-air. Between these intervals of complete union with God, he worked on perfecting the rules of his Order, condensing and simplifying them and making them more specific. He would issue from his cell only for Mass and Communion and to pick up his meager helpings of fruit and vegetables. He would also accept visits from his royal and clerical admirers.

Back in 1493, Pope Alexander VI had by Papal decree approved the title for the Congregation that Francis had submitted, along with a new draft of rules. The title "Order of the Minimi" ("Order of the Least") describes graphically what Francis had in mind as a teenager when he lived in the cave outside his home town of Paola. Before the name "Minimi" became the official designation of the Congregation, the Hermit Friars in Calabria were called the "Hermits of Paola;" in Genoa, "The Friars of Prince d'Oria;" in Tours, *"Les Bon Hommes"* ("The Good Men"); in Tolouse, *"Rochettes"* ("Cogs"); and in Spain, "The Brothers of Victory." The Spanish designation grew out of the appearance of the Saint's emissaries, Fathers Bernardino di Cropalati and Jaime Lespervier, at the Spanish royal court of Ferdinand and Isabella during the siege of Malaga in 1483. The two Hermit Friars had delivered a prophetic message from the Calabrian Holy Man, advising them to press the siege, as God would give them victory in a short while. Within a few days the Moors' defense collapsed and they surrendered, ending forever the Moorish rule over Spain.

The Pope's sanction of this title, Order of the Minimi, was of particular satisfaction to the Calabrian Holy Man. Thereafter he closed his letters signing them "The poor friar Francis of Paola, the least of the least servants of Blessed Jesus Christ."

The rules approved by Pope Alexander VI in 1493 were thirteen in number. The first covers the vows of perpetual poverty, chastity and obedience. The second requires full

obedience to the Roman Pontiff and to the superiors
("correctors") of the monasteries, with a cardinal appointed by the Pope as their protector at the Holy See.
The third rule concerns the divine office, outlining specific prayers to be said at certain times each day. The
fourth rule states that the clothing of the Hermit Friars
shall be of black lamb's wool, the tunic reaching to the
shins, a hood over the head and a black rope of the same
material around the waist. Sandals were to be worn, with
shoes permitted during inclement weather.

The fifth rule establishes the diet that all Minimi members must follow, except those who were under doctor's
care (and even in such cases the diet had to be restricted).
For the able-bodied, the fare would be that of a perpetual
fast. The sixth rule denies members personal possession of
money, the seventh, abstinence from food, not only on the
regular days of abstinence set aside by the Church, but on
all Wednesdays and Fridays of the year, and on the Feast
days of All Saints and Christmas. Also, the Minimi priests,
in addition to prayers at Mass, were to participate in special prayers at other hours of the day. The eighth rule imposes strict silence during certain hours and in certain
locations, and the manner in which strangers and other religious must be addressed.

The ninth rule requires spiritual readings at all meals,
forbids the acceptance from lay people of invitations to
dine, and imposes the duty that everyone be treated with
charity. The tenth rule requires daily Confession and
Communion, plus every Monday, Wednesday and Friday
an open review of sins and temptations.

The eleventh rule requires all friars to leave the monastery in pairs, only after obtaining the consent of the corrector, to avoid idle talk with the people or the clergy encountered anywhere, and instead of being critical of
others, to meditate on their own unworthiness. The twelfth
rule outlines the punishment for those who violate religious vows or the rules of the Order, and in the final rule,
the government of the Order is outlined. The head of each

monastery shall be known as "corrector," instead of superior, and he must set a strict example for the friars under his care in behavior, speech, and supervision, punishing wrong-doers with understanding and charity.

In approving the thirteen rules, the Pope nominated the Spanish cardinal Bernardino Lopez de Carvajal, Titular Bishop of Jerusalem, as the first Protector. In 1503, the Cardinal was a leading candidate for the Papacy. With the help of Father Binet he rewrote and condensed the thirteen rules into ten and resubmitted them for approval. One change related to a distinction in the dress between novices and regular members. This new set of rules met with the ready approval of the Pope. However, Francis was not satisfied with receiving the approval of the Pope alone. He wanted the approval of the College of Cardinals, so he prepared a third version, covering the same ground as the first two versions, but putting special emphasis on the need for religious perfection. The new rules were submitted to the Pope through Cardinal Carvajal as Protector. The Cardinal explained to the Pope the Saint's desire. Alexander promptly agreed and convened the cardinals. The Cardinal Protector read the rules to the assembled cardinals, who readily gave their endorsement, and they were immediately issued under the Papal seal on May 18, 1502.

With the passing of Alexander VI on August 18, 1503, and his short-lived successor Pius III, who died after reigning less than one month, Francis, at a request from Spain, expanded the Order to cover women who felt the divine urge to live lives of penance, self-mortification and solitude. Giuliano della Rovere was elected to the Papal throne on October 31, 1503, taking the name Julius II. As a cardinal he had been deeply impressed by the piety and miraculous powers of the great Hermit Friar, and when the Calabrian submitted a fourth version of the rules, including rules for a cloistered order of nuns and minor order for lay-people, along with certain disciplinary changes, the new Pope turned them over to the theologians and canonists for evaluation. They approved the text, which was then submitted to a convocation of the cardinals, with the Pope presiding. Here again it won unanimous approval and was again published under the Papal seal on July 18, 1506. These are the rules that are in force in all Minimi monasteries today.

Advising the Calabrian Saint about the blanket approval of the fourth set of rules for his Order, Julius II also extended certain special privileges, including the burial of lay people, who asked for this privilege, in the chapels of the Minimi, so that they could enjoy all the spiritual benefits that accrue to the Order. The Pope also granted the Minimi the privilege of ordaining priests at the early age of twenty-two. These rules won the praise of subsequent Popes. Clement VII, who succeeded to the Papacy in 1525, wrote: "Francis of Paola, although lacking literary training, inspired by the Holy Spirit, composed a set of rules which are the most comprehensive and perfect for a religious existence." The Calabrian himself referred to these rules as the practice of "evangelical penance," for in his concept, penance was basic to a holy and useful life.

The second Order of the Minimi, that of the nuns, was instituted, strangely enough, in Spain in 1495 by two nieces of the Spanish Ambassador at Tours. They were living at Andujar, a town east of Cordoba.

They had heard of the Calabrian Holy Man through their uncle's letters. The Ambassador was Count Pedro of Lucena Olit. The two founders were Maria and Francesca Valencuola. They were deeply impressed by Francis' miracles and his dedication to prayer, penance and self-mortification, and they wanted to emulate him. Father Germano Lionnet and his fellow Hermit Friars, who had been sent by Francis to the Court of Ferdinand and Isabella, were guests of the Court of Lucena. The two young ladies sought them out and asked many questions about the Minimi and the possible creation of a women's branch. When this suggestion was transmitted to the Calabrian Saint at Tours, he endorsed the idea enthusiastically. In the meantime, the two young ladies secluded themselves in the most austere room in the castle and devoted their time to prayer and meditation, living on a simple diet. Soon, several other young ladies asked to join them, and at the end of 1488, through the good offices of their uncle, the Spanish Ambassador, they requested approval from the Calabrian Holy Man to be recognized as the women's branch of his Order. The Saint wrote them:

"To the devout daughters secluded in the house of the Most Excellent Don Pedro of Lucena Olid, wishing to found a monastery:

"My sisters, I am greatly comforted by how dearly you hold your vocation, as indicated by the letter to our good father, Don Pedro of Lucena. Only God can sanctify you and the souls to be made holy through your example. Your good founder will inform you of the requirements for women I have transmitted to him, and also [about] the prayers that should be repeated daily for peace [and] concord among Christian princes, so essential for everyone, because if God does not treat us with saintly mercy, we shall suffer great miseries. Pray therefore to God fervently for this boon. Peace is a holy merchandise that must be bought at a great price. Work constantly to sanctify yourselves inwardly, that you may become precious to God and be worthy to receive from Him all that you ask. Ask also for the physical and spiritual well-being of your founder (Father Germain Lionnet) and in your prayers of your poor brother, Friar Francis of Paola, the least of the least servants of the Blessed Jesus Christ. Tours, January 21, 1489."

The two sisters and their companions continued their pious self-denial and seclusion for six years. On June 11, 1495, the Feast of St. Barnabas, they received their monastic habits from Father Lionnet, who designated Father John Bois as their corrector. The monastery of Jesus and Mary was erected for them in Andujar, the first for the new order of women Minimi. The Calabrian Saint was tremendously pleased and grateful to witness this new congregation come into being, seeing it as the will of God for the sanctification of more souls. On January 15, 1501, Francis wrote to the girls' uncle, telling him that he was working on rules for the nuns. He wrote:

"With the help of God, we will provide for their holy intention, so that, joined in charity and piety under your roof, and living according to rules of our religion, they will be able to instruct other women by prayers and example."

A year later, with the monastery at Andujar completed, the nuns requested from the Saint rules that would be of particular use to them. They referred to him as the "Most reverend, devout and desired Father in Jesus Christ" and referred to themselves as "your most humble Minimi." Francis hesitated imposing rules as harsh as those he had laid down for men. He was also concerned about the danger of daily relationship between his friars and members of the new branch, which could scandalize the Order and the Church. Under the rules he finally drafted, the monasteries would be under the direction of a female corrector; no woman was to be accepted under the age of twenty-five; and all were to serve a two-year novitiate, against one year for men, before receiving final investiture. The habit was to be of the same cloth as for the friars, black lamb's wool, with a black veil covering the head and face. The novices were to wear a band around the head and waist, instead of the black hood and rope cincture. The nuns were to be isolated from the friars by double grates covered with black veils, and could not leave their cloisters except to be transferred to other monasteries. Their food and other needs would be filled by the friars, under strict supervision. The confessors were to be selected by the correctors, provincials, or the general of the First Order, and had to be over fifty years of age. However, confessors for the friars themselves had to be at least forty years of age, under the assumption that no one less than that age had sufficient understanding of life and of sin to counsel sinners properly.

In 1501, Francis also clarified and made official the rules for a Third Order, covering lay men and women who had to continue their life in the world, yet who wanted to receive the special spiritual benefits of the Order. Even before he left Calabria, long before he decided to establish the Third Order along the lines of St. Francis of Assisi's Third Order, he had given his blessing to a group of pious lay admirers in Altilia, near Cosenza, who wanted to follow a life of charity, prayer and self-denial. The rules of this Third Order require that the members recite special daily prayers, receive Communion at least four times a year, and purify and beautify their souls by frequent Confession, meditation and penance. The four days on which Communion was to be received were either Holy Thursday or Easter Sunday, Christmas Day, Pentecost, and the Assumption of the Blessed Virgin Mary. Later, four more Communion days were added, The Purification of the Blessed Virgin (February 2), the Feast of St. Michael the Archangel, the Feast of All Saints, and the Feast of the Founder of the Minimi.

Members of the Third Order were to consider their bedrooms as cells, and retire to them daily for periods of prayer, examination of conscience and meditation. They were also required to practice charity in all dealings with others.

The final rules for the First, Second and Third Orders of the Minimi were formally approved by a convocation of cardinals, with the Pope presiding, and were distributed throughout the Christian World under the Pope's Seal on July 28, 1506.

Chapter 24

THE DEATH OF A SAINT

With the beginning of 1507, Francis became aware that his end was approaching. However, he continued his rigid self-mortification, sleeping on a bed of dried grape vines, with his head resting on a large stone. His only covering was the tunic and hood he wore constantly. He slept in a cell with the minimum of heat. Despite his age and growing infirmity, he continued his strict diet of fruit and vegetables, cooked in the simplest way possible. Each three hours he would awaken for his regular periods of prayer and meditation. As we have indicated, his moments of ecstacy, when he appeared to be transported completely out of the world of reality, became more frequent and more intense. And despite his growing difficulty in moving about, he persisted in making his routine rounds.

While he was deeply concerned with the progress and effectiveness of the First Order of Friars and the Second Order of Nuns, that they pursue the strict rules he had outlined for the Minimi, he also gave considerable time and thought to the Third Order for lay followers. He wanted them to observe faithfully simple but effective religious practices. The first of these practices was the devotion of the Thirteen Fridays, symbolizing Christ and His twelve Apostles, when every member was to confess all his sins and faults and to receive Holy Communion. During the Mass they were to recite thirteen Our Fathers and thirteen Hail Marys while thinking of Christ and His twelve disciples. Also they were to light two candles, one for faith and the other for hope, and hold a third lighted candle in their hands, signifying Christian charity. Thus, he said, will God grant you your just deserts. Francis was born on a Friday, and that apparently accounted for his selecting that day. Furthermore, he dedicated himself completely to the service of God when he was thirteen, a symbolic age that, he felt, was preordained. Pope Clement VII, one of the Calabrian Saint's most ardent admirers, was particularly impressed with the Thirteen Fridays devotion, and granted a seven-year indulgence for the faithful who fulfilled the requirements. Later, Benedict XIV extended the indulgence to forty years, and in 1928 Pius XI made it a plenary indulgence if the faithful would add prayers for cooperation among Christian leaders for the eradication of heresies and the success of the Church.

With an awareness of the approaching end of his earthly existence, the Saint, always calm and serene, became even more so. As his ninety-first birthday approached, March 27, 1507, he quietly informed his Hermit Friars that his end was imminent. During the Lenten period he had developed a slight fever, which affected his movements. It made him weaker and interfered greatly with carrying out his established routine, but he forced himself to continue it. On March 28, Palm Sunday, his fever had become so high as to make his every move extremely difficult, but still he persisted, refusing to take long rests, or to abandon any of his activities. On the morning of Holy Thursday he called together all the Hermit Friars in the Tours area to give them final instructions and his blessing. He asked that they be faithful to the rules of the Order and zealous in saving their souls and those of the people who sought their spiritual help, that they observe strictly the fast and abstinence required by the Order, and that they promote the Order throughout the Christian world.

As he finished speaking, the brazier that was used to heat the room, having become overheated, burst into flames. The friars moved away from the flaming receptacle, but the Calabrian walked over to the brazier and picked it up from the floor with his bare hands, saying: "Be assured, my brothers, that it is not difficult for one who truly loves God to carry out what He wishes, which for me is holding in my hands this fire."

He held it flaming around his hands and arms, until some friars brought in bricks to make a platform on which he placed it. When the ordeal was over, the friars present fell on their knees, and weeping, promised the Saint that they would faithfully fulfill all of their obligations.

Francis then fell to his knees and confessed in a clear voice that at times he had not been as zealous as he should have been and that he did not always give a demonstration of religious and spiritual perfection. With tears in his eyes, he begged the Almighty to forgive him. The friars each made the same confession aloud. They then arose and came to their patriarch, weeping unashamedly, for a last embrace and personal blessing.

Supported by the superior and other friars, they then went with him to Mass. Here he fell on his knees, placing the rope he wore around his waist around his neck. He recited, as was the custom with the Minimi, the prayer to the Holy Trinity of St. Gregory, the poet-saint. With deep humility and piety, he received the Holy Eucharist and joined in the singing. At the end of Mass, he became extremely weak and the friars carried him to his cell and placed him on his crude bedding.

In the afternoon, though obviously weaker, the Calabrian Saint painfully returned to the chapel to participate in the Holy Thursday ceremony of the washing of the feet. The Father Corrector wanted to start the washing ceremony with him, but the Saint insisted that he begin with the others, and that he, "Il minimo dei minimi" ("The least of the least"), should be last. He added: "Son, wait until tomorrow and you will wash not only my feet, but my body and head."

After the ceremony, he again asked his friars always to live in peace and harmony and in the charity of Jesus Christ. He was then assisted by the friars into his cell, conscious that the end of his earthly existence was only a short time away. Prostrated on his bed of vines, he asked for the

Last Rites, and having received them, he composed himself peacefully, closing his eyes. Brother Bertre was left to maintain a vigil. During the night he was heard to moan and sigh, but he was far too weak to make an effort to follow his nightly routine of prayer and meditation.

The next morning, unable to rise from his bed, he asked that Father Bernardino Otranto da Cropalati, his confessor, Father Jacques Lespervier, the corrector at the Plessis monastery, and Father Matthew Michel gather in his cell. He told them that he wanted to name his successor as the head of the Minimi. He then designated Father Bernardino to succeed him. Father Bernardino protested that he was unworthy and unfit for such a charge, but the Saint waved away his objections. The Founder assured him that God would guide him and give him superhuman wisdom in directing the Order, as He would for all other successors. He also discussed the holding of a general meeting of the Order in Rome.

With these technical matters out of the way, he asked that the penitential Psalms be read and then participated in the Litany of the Saints. He also requested that the Gospel of St. John relating to the Passion of Christ be read to him. During these activities, he continued to cross himself with Holy Water and kiss a crucifix, murmuring: "Into thy hands, O Father, I consign my soul." Those in his cell were on their knees, praying fervently with tears in their eyes, overcome with grief, while the other friars in the monastery had gathered in the chapel and knelt in prayer. About 10 a.m., the Saint in a loud voice said: "O my Lord Jesus Christ! O Good Shepherd, save the just, reclaim sinners, have mercy on all the faithful, living and dead, and on me, a miserable sinner. Amen."

He then spoke the name of Jesus and Mary, and with a deep sigh, passed away.

A great hush fell on the assembled holy men, broken only by occasional sobs. It was Good Friday, April 2, 1507, the anniversary of the death of the Savior he loved so deeply. He was ninety-one years and six days old. He had lived longer by many years than most of the saints of the Church, and had willingly and completely committed himself to a life of religious dedication and self-mortification at an earlier age than almost any other saint. Those in the cell were stunned with grief at the passing of their spiritual father—a completely committed servant of God.

Father Michael Lecomte, corrector of the Monastery at Gien, who was present at the death of the Saint, was assigned the task of preparing the text of the notice of his passing. It was written in Latin and read:

"The Founder and First Corrector General of the Order of the Minimi, Brother Francis of Paola, our good father, died in our presence the Second of April, 1507, about 10 o'clock in the morning. May his soul rest in peace. Amen.

"This occurred in our monastery at Montils and his last words were: 'O My Lord Jesus Christ, O good Shepherd, save the just, reclaim sinners, have mercy on all the faithful, living and dead, and on me, a miserable sinner. Amen. Jesus! Mary!' "

Father Lecomte, with many others present, heard the Saint with his last breath repeat three times: "Lord, into thy hands I commend my spirit."

Though dead, the Calabrian Holy Man seemed to the friars who filed in simply to have fallen into a peaceful sleep. Each one knelt in front of the body as if before an altar, to pay their last respects. There was something majestic about his body; his face, pale before, regained its color, and his features settled into a look of triumph.

The Father Corrector asked the wife of Hilaire Bonhomme, the village blacksmith, to advise the people of the neighborhood about the death of the Saint and to ask help in arranging a funeral for the Holy Man. The court artist, John Bourdichon, was charged with making a death mask of the Saint. That evening, the body, placed in a wooden casket made by the court carpenter, Michael Treloppe, was placed in the chapel, where it remained for three days.

Thousands from the surrounding area of France filed by the coffin and gazed at the body with deep veneration. Some kissed the hands that had produced such numerous miracles and had comforted so many and prayed for his continuous intercession from beyond the grave.

The crowd became so numerous and so eager to kiss and touch the Saint and to take away some relic that the friars had to ask the King for a platoon of soldiers to control those who were too zealous. In spite of the soldiers, the hair coat he wore under his tunic, the rope he wore around his waist, and most of his tunic were torn and snatched away by people who believed in their miraculous powers.

Jeanne Loyon, four-year-old daughter of the Prefect of the Forests of the Queen, was suffering from a tumor on the face which had blinded her left eye. The best doctors of the court were unable to help the unfortunate child. Her mother, a pious woman named Catherine, knowing of the miraculous powers of the Saint, and that he himself had been cured of a similar condition when a child, took her daughter to the chapel so that she could touch the body of the Calabrian Miracle Worker, saying: "If he is truly blessed in Heaven, he will restore the vision of my daughter, Jeanne."

They arrived just as the friars were preparing to close the coffin. The friars permitted the child to touch the Saint, while her mother invoked the intercession of the departed Servant of God. No sooner had Jeanne touched the body than her sight was restored.

While the friars were finishing nailing down the coffin, a widow, Jeanne Beauvalet, who had fallen off a horse, and had been badly injured, hurried into the chapel and begged the friars in the name of Charity to reopen the coffin so that she too could touch the Calabrian Holy Man's body. They obliged. She touched the body and then knelt at the altar in prayer. When she arose, she was completely whole again.

Easter Monday, on order from the King, the coffin was to be placed in the vault in the wall of the chapel on the right side of the altar. The coffin was lowered into the opening during a ceremony in which all the clergy, secular and regular, in the area of Tours and Amboise, participated. A turnout of believers packed the chapel, with hundreds kneeling in prayer outside the church. The stones were put into place and sealed by two of the court masons, Michel Marseil and Jean Bussiere.

However, the body was to remain in the vault only a few days. The Duchess of Angouleme, Louise of Savoy, worried because the chapel, close to the River Cher, was flooded from time to time. She requested that she be permitted to have a waterproof tomb built of bricks so that the humidity would not affect the body. On Thursday, April 8, three days after the depositing of the body in the vault, it was lifted out and opened under the personal supervision of the Duchess of Savoy. It was found that the body and face were as fresh as at the moment of death and that there was no indication of rigor mortis; the hands and arms were limber, and he appeared to be in a pleasant sleep. No sign of decay was present. The court artist Bourdichon made a second death mask for comparison with the first.

To build a waterproof resting place, a mammoth stone was transported from the parish of Ballan, some three kilometers from Tours. The first attempt by the owner, a commander of the Knights of Malta, to move this massive stone failed to budge it, though he used eighteen pairs of bulls. At the suggestion of former Queen Anne of France, several Minimi friars with a team of five horses were able to transport the huge rock without difficulty to the chapel and put it in place where the body could be kept, at least one foot above the water and within a water-tight vault. This was accomplished on Tuesday, April 13, eleven days after the death of the great Calabrian. A simple stone lid on which was carved a likeness of the Saint was placed over the vault.

For fifty-five years the Saint's tomb attracted a steady stream of devout persons and became a pilgrimage site equal in the minds of French Catholics to that of the Patron Saint of France, St. Martin.

Then, as Francis had predicted so many years before, heresy flamed. Catherine de Medici, as regent for her son, the ten-year-old Charles IX, under the guise of religious liberty, insisted on maintaining a neutral attitude in the struggle between Catholics and the Protestant Huguenots. However, in January, 1562, Catherine had a change of heart and ordered the Huguenots to repair the damages to churches and properties of Catholics and to reimburse them for their losses. This infuriated the Protestants. Bands of Huguenots roamed through France burning churches, monasteries and convents, and desecrating tombs of saints. One of the first tombs attacked was that of St. Martin in Tours, where they burned his remains.

On April 13, 1562, the Huguenots broke into the chapel at Montils, ripped open the tomb in which the Calabrian Saint was buried, and though finding the body still incorrupt, snatched it out of its coffin, carried it to the nearby forester lodge, and burned the remains in the fireplace on a fire of coal and wood. In the course of their attack on the chapel, they threw down a flight of stairs and killed Father Eustache Apuril, an eighty-four-year old Minimi priest, who was trying to stop them. When the Catholics regained control of the area, they were able to salvage many bones and other relics of the Saint. In fact, some Catholics, mixing in among the rioting Protestants, were able to save parts of the Saint's arms and legs and clothing.

The Duke of Montpensier, Louis of Bourbon, recovered Tours from the Huguenots, and by the first of July the Minimi were back in their devastated monastery at Montils. The desecrators were hung in the main square of Tours, and their goods sold to pay for the restoration of the damage they had caused. The remains of the Saint that were found were placed in the tomb. In 1630, a new and more impressive tomb of marble was erected, five feet above the floor, and dedicated with a solemn ceremony in the presence of representatives of the Catholic royal house, the nobility, and the Catholic hierarchy of France. The tomb contains thirteen bones of the Saint—six vertebrae (three from the cervical and three from the lumbar regions), the sacrum, a fragment of a tibia, the two temporals, two parts of a hip bone, plus a small unidentified piece of bone—along with pieces of his tunic, his bed of vines, and a piece of the rope he wore around his waist. Other relics of the Saint were taken by devout followers and are found in churches and monasteries in France, Spain, and Italy.

Over the years, the tomb was visited not only by hundreds of devout pilgrims, but also by several French kings, Henry III, Henry IV, Louis XIII, and Louis XIV (*Le Roi Soleil*—The Sun King), also by Catherine de Medici, Anne of Austria, and Louise of Lorraine. During the French Revolution, the chapel and the tomb were again destroyed. Both were restored in 1957 thanks to Friends of St. Francis of Paola, organized by Raoul Lohoux, superintendent of monuments for the region of Tours, with the help of the Marquis Wladimir D'Ormesson, French Ambassador to the Holy See. The tomb of the Saint is enclosed in a glass frame on which is carved in Latin his name and a summary of his achievements. Pilgrims from Calabria, Naples, and other parts of Italy, from France and from Spain visit the chapel and tomb each year.

Chapter 25

CANONIZATION

Queen Anne of France, wife of Louis XII, a long-time and devoted follower of the Calabrian Saint, took the initiative in having him canonized. She was actuated by the miraculous cure of her daughter, Princess Claude, from a devastating fever through the intercession of the deceased Saint.

At the end of April, 1507, the very month the Calabrian Holy Man had passed away, the young Princess developed a mysterious fever, which made her steadily weaker. The best doctors of France, despite all their efforts, were unable to help the unfortunate Princess. When the Queen, at that time staying at the royal castle near Grenoble, heard of her daughter's mysterious illness, she became alarmed and rushed to Tours. The doctors, with due regret and deference, advised her that there was nothing more that they could do for the Princess. The devoted mother was overcome with grief for her only child. She was not only a model child but also of major importance to the future of the royal house.

The Queen turned to Lawrence Cardinal Allemand, Archbishop of Grenoble, her father confessor and one of the oldest friends and admirers of the Calabrian Miracle Worker. (His admiration stemmed from the day the Saint passed through Grenoble in 1483 on his way to King Louis XI.) The Cardinal hurried to Tours at the Queen's urgent request, but all his efforts and exhortations were unable to comfort her. Then he recalled the many miracles worked by the Calabrian Holy Man, who had just died and was undoubtedly among the saints in Heaven. The Queen had often seen the Saint at the royal court, on the palace grounds, and at Mass and had always treated him with reverence. The Calabrian, as was his habit, had spoken to her many times. Always a good Catholic, she quickly hurried into the chapel at the Montils Monastery, where the Holy Man was buried. Earnestly she pleaded with the departed Saint to cure her daughter from this terrible fever, promising that if he did she would initiate immediately the cause of his canonization. The next day, while Cardinal Allemand was trying to comfort the Queen, a messenger arrived to tell them that the fever had left her daughter and that she was fully conscious again and anxious to see her mother.

Overcome with joy, the Queen hurried to her daughter's bedside, and finding her completely restored, embraced her happily, murmuring prayers of thanks to the departed Saint for this great miracle and fervently promising to launch the canonization efforts immediately.

True to her word, she wrote to Julius II, a Pope thoroughly familiar with the works of the Saint and his humble devotion to God and the Church. She also wrote to all members of the French hierarchy and nobility, requesting them to support her proposal. She urged the Holy Father to begin immediate hearings in France and Italy to authenticate the saintliness and miraculous works performed by the Calabrian Man of God in these two countries. She expressly charged Robert Cardinal Guibe, former Bishop of Nantes, resident in Rome, to prevail on the Pope to take the necessary steps to achieve canonization as quickly as possible. The Queen's request was naturally supported enthusiastically by the Minimi through their Procurator General, Father Francis Binet, and fully endorsed by Cardinal Protector Carvajal, the Pope's appointee to oversee the operations of the Minimi. Father Binet urged speed in convoking hearings because of the Saint's great age at his death. He pointed out that many of those who had been beneficiaries of his miraculous powers, as well as those who had been witness to them, were extremely old and feeble and in danger of death.

Recognizing this urgency, Pope Julius issued a brief on May 13, 1512, ordering bishops in France and Italy to initiate hearings on the life, virtues, and miracles of the founder of the Minimi, and asking them to carry out his request promptly, faithfully and with all due care. In France, this brief was forwarded to the Bishop of Paris, Mgr. Stephen Poncher, the Bishop of Grenoble, Cardinal Allemand, and to the Bishop of Auxerre, Mgr. John Baillet. Unfortunately, the last of these died on November 10, 1513, before he could fulfill his assignment.

Bishop Poncher of Paris, a native of Tours, who was well acquainted with the Saint's achievements and holiness and was most anxious to support the Queen in her endeavor, was forced to delegate his responsibility to subordinates because he had been appointed Minister of the King's Seals, a political office that required all his time and attention. Two of the three to whom the bishop delegated this responsibility were Fathers Peter Chabrion and Peter Cruchet, both canons of the Cathedral of Tours. The third was Stephen Chanton, an official of Tours.

The personal representative of Cardinal Allemand, James Tillier, a notary of Tours, was named as the presiding officer for the hearings. The public hearings began on July 10, 1513 (several months being necessary to notify possible witnesses), and ended on September 7, 1513. The commission listened to the testimony of fifty-seven witnesses, persons who themselves had been beneficiaries of the Saint's miraculous powers or had been personal observers of such acts. Records of the two months of hearings, taken in French, were submitted to the Bishop of Paris for review, authentication, and translation into Latin. On April 14, 1514, the Bishop forwarded them to Pope Leo X, with an earnest plea for the speedy canonization of the Calabrian Holy Man. This hearing is known in Italian as *"Processo Turonense"* ("The Hearing of Tours").

Some months earlier, June 2, 1512, at the request of Queen Anne, Father Giulio had transmitted the Papal brief to Mgr. John Sersale, Bishop of Cariati, Calabria, and Mgr. Benardin Cavalcanti, canon of the diocese of Cosenza. They were to invite witnesses of the Saint's holiness and miraculous acts from all sections of Calabria. The hearing at Cosenza, called *"Processo Cosentino,"* started June 15, 1512, and continued through January 18, 1513, with a total of 103 witnesses being heard. The proceedings were recorded in the Calabrian dialect, the common language of the witnesses, by the Archdeacon of Cariati, Nicolo Sproviero. These were later translated into Latin by Sigismund Pindaro, the secretary of Lorenzo Cardinal Pucci. Cardinal Pucci presided over the hearings as the representative of Cardinal Carvajal, the official representative of the Order of the Minimi in the College of Cardinals.

Mgr. Francis D'Allevyn, delegate of the Bishop of Paris, held a hearing at Amiens on June 13, 1513, to take down the testimony of a single witness, a certain Anthony di Jerana di Figline, a Calabrian merchant then living in Amiens.

While work was in progress to compile the proceedings of the hearings at Cosenza *(Processo Cosentino)*, Pope Julius died unexpectedly on February 21, 1513. Less than two weeks later, March 3, John Cardinal de Medici, a long-time, devoted friend and admirer of the Calabrian Holy Man, was elected to the Papal throne as Leo X. It will be recalled that in March, 1483, while Francis was in Rome on his way to France, Lorenzo de Medici, ruler of Florence, took his seven-year-old son John to pay respects to the Calabrian Miracle Worker. As John kissed the Saint's hand, the Calabrian embraced him and said to him prophetically: "I shall be a saint when you become Pope!"

Pope Leo gave the canonization of the great Saint special attention, taking a personal interest in its progress. Four months after he had been elevated to the Papacy, Leo issued a decree declaring the Calabrian Holy Man Blessed. The decree established April 2, the date of the Saint's passing, as his Feast day, and the Minimi were instructed to offer special ceremonial Masses on that date. Queen Anne was greatly pleased over Pope Leo's action and doubled her efforts for canonization.

However, progress toward early canonization received a twin setback when Cardinal Guibe, the former Bishop of Nantes, who represented Queen Anne on behalf of the canonization process at the Vatican, died on November 9, 1513, and then the Queen herself, who had devoted so much time and energy to this enterprise, passed away suddenly at the age of 33 on January 4, 1514. King Louis XII, though weighed down by affairs of state, still managed to devote attention to promoting his dead Queen's life ambition to have the Holy Man made a saint at the earliest possible moment. Louis had hesitated to get too involved in the canonization action before because of a long-standing feud with then Pope Julius II. When he assumed the throne of France, Louis had given his backing to the antipapal council held in Pisa, which created great problems and embarrassment for Julius II. However, Louis and the French Royal House had been on good terms with the Medicis in Florence, and when Lorenzo's son became Pope, Louis' enmity with the Holy See disappeared. In fact, he was pleased to have an opportunity to ingratiate himself with Leo X and his powerful Florentine family. Unfortunately, the French King too was struck down suddenly at age 53 on January 1, 1515, a year after the passing of his devout Queen, and three months after he had married the sister of the notorious King of England, Henry VIII. He was succeeded by his cousin, the Count of Angouleme, who had married the only child of Louis XII and Queen Anne, Princess Claude, miraculously cured of a near-fatal fever by the Saint.

Claude's husband took the name of Francis I. He was only 21, but was courteous and considerate. The son of Louise of Savoy, he had deep respect for the Saint. His feelings toward the Calabrian Holy Man were more than shared by Queen Claude, eternally grateful to the dead Saint for the miracle that had saved her life.

King Francis had indicated his deep dedication to the
Minimi even before he succeeded to the throne. In a letter
patent dated December 7, 1514, the Prince had declared
the Minimi of Tours and Amboise exempt from whatever
taxes related to food, travel, and other necessities. He
granted these immunities not only because of the austere
life led by the Hermit Monks but also because of their concern for and care of the sick and poor. Once enthroned as
King of France, Francis himself turned to the deceased
Saint to ask for a special favor. Queen Claude had given
him two daughters, whom he cherished deeply, but he
wanted a male heir. In the presence of members of his
royal court, the King knelt and prayed to the Calabrian
Holy Man to intercede in obtaining for him a son. When
the King made his fervent and unusual public appeal, the
Corrector General of the Minimi, Father Binet, was present. The King promised in his prayers that he would make
every possible effort to speed the departed Saint's canonization. Confident that the Saint would fulfill his plea, he
did not wait for it to be realized. He and Queen Claude
wrote letters to Leo X and the College of Cardinals, begging them to hurry the canonization process. Three letters from the King and five from the Queen on this subject
were sent to the Pope during the first year of Francis' reign,
1516. Altogether there are extant more than fifteen letters
sent from the royal couple to the Pope up to the date of the
actual canonization. The Holy Man fulfilled their solemn
request. On February 28, 1518, the Queen gave birth to the
much wanted Dauphin. The young Prince was baptized in
an impressive ceremony at the royal palace, with the
Pope's nephew, Lorenzo de Medici, acting as proxy god-
father for the Pontiff. In honor of the great Saint, he too
was baptized "Francis."

The King and Queen, impressed by the fulfillment of
their prayers, redoubled their efforts to have the Hermit
canonized. They urged all the members of the royal
family, the French heirarchy, and the nobility to write to
the Vatican. Filiberte, Duchess of Savoy, wrote a particu-

larly memorable letter to the Pope on this matter on December 10, 1516.

At the same time, the clergy, nobles, and common people of Calabria were pressing energetically for the canonization of the amazing Calabrian Wonder Worker. Many eagerly reported miracles that the Holy Man had performed on their behalf or for relatives and friends. Among the letters urging his speedy canonization, there is one from the University of Paola. While these appeals were being considered by the Pope, another miracle was performed by the Saint.

A certain Julius Bertuccio was supervising the transportation of a large cannon from the castle at Cosenza to Paola. The piece was being pulled by twenty bulls. The party reached a certain point where it was necessary to lower the cannon down a hillside with ropes. A running noose was arranged around a huge tree. The men were letting the cannon down the slope when one of the ropes slipped, and as the weight of the piece of artillery pulled the rope rapidly, Bertuccio tried to grasp it. But it wound around his leg and started to pull him down at an ever increasing speed, while his companions watched helplessly. Thoroughly frightened, he was heard to shout: "O Blessed Francis of Paola, save me!" Immediately the rope stopped pulling, and Julius was able to get to his feet unhurt. He later stated that during his frightful ordeal he thought he saw a friar in a Minimi tunic and hood, grasping the rope and holding it while he was able to free himself. The rescuer was apparently the Calabrian Holy Man himself. All of Bertuccio's companions were amazed at the happening and joined Julius at the nearby Minimi Chapel at Paola to thank God and the Blessed Francis for this miracle.

This event occurred during the fourth series of hearings, called the *"Processo Calabro"* ("Calabrian Hearings"), which started in 1516 and ended in 1518. These hearings covered 120 new witnesses, in addition to those who had been interviewed earlier at Tours, Amiens, and Cosenza.

The proceedings of the four independent hearings, once translated into Latin, were submitted by the Pope to his cardinals for study and recommendation. Three cardinals prepared the report, whole-heartedly endorsing the canonization. On May 1, 1519, with the Catholic world's foremost religious leaders present, with political representation from all of Europe, and in one of the most memorable ceremonial Masses in Church history, the Pope solemnly announced that Francis of Paola had been officially inscribed in the Book of Saint Confessors, that his Feast was to be celebrated on April 2, and that the faithful should not only implore his intercession but also render him special honor. Thus did the "Least of the Least" become a major saint of the Church he had so faithfully and single-heartedly served all his life.

Few saints had been canonized so soon after their deaths, and one might question if any had ever performed so many miracles that were so thoroughly and completely authenticated, or had had such an influence on the history of Europe, particularly of France. St. Francis helped shape the thinking and policy of four major kings of France along more Christian lines, despite their tendency toward despotism and self-indulgence, so typical of rulers of that day.

In the canonization decree, Pope Leo granted a plenary indulgence to all the faithful who visited the tomb of the Saint on his feast day, April 2, and lesser indulgences for honoring him at lesser places.

Francis had lived during the reign of twelve Popes. His birth at this particular moment in the history of the Catholic Church, and certainly his life, self denial, and miraculous achievements had great, even if subtle, influence on the historic Council of Trent (1545-1563), some twenty-five years after his canonization, a council which clarified forever the basic theological and moral doctrines of the Catholic Church.

Chapter 26

THE SAINT THROUGH THE AGES

At the time that the great Calabrian Miracle Worker died, there were thirty-three Minimi monasteries and convents in existence. In France, where he spent the last twenty-four years of his life, they numbered fourteen. In his native land, Italy, there were twelve, six of them in Calabria. There were four in Spain, two in Germany, and one in Bohemia, founded by missionaries sent out from his headquarters monastery at Montils. Also in France, three monasteries were under construction at the time of his death.

After his passing, new Minimi monasteries and convents were built in increasing numbers. Toward the end of the seventeenth century, the total number of Hermit Friars was reported at more than 12,000 in almost 500 monasteries in the countries listed above and in Belgium, Portugal and the New World. Minimi monasteries had been built on the Island of Majorca and in all areas of France, Italy, Spain, Germany and Belgium, and also in faraway Peru on the Pacific coast of South America. They were grouped into thirty-two provinces, covering separate facilities for friars and nuns. The first province is coterminous with the Calabrian political province of Cosenza.

The growth of new monasteries continued uninterrupted for 300 years, until the French Revolution. Many of the monasteries were wantonly destroyed by anti-Catholic revolutionary mobs. When Napoleon became First Consul after crushing the controlling Directory, and despite his pretense at being a Catholic, he issued a decree on April 25, 1800, suppressing religious orders throughout France and those parts of Italy under his control. When, after the famous retreat from Moscow in 1812, Napoleon was forced finally into exile on the Island of Elba in 1814, Pius VII was able to restore the Minimi monasteries and convents, but Napoleon's senseless decree had greatly damaged the Order during the fourteen years it was in force.

The Calabrian Saint's miraculous powers continued to operate after his death. In Amiens, France, on Good Friday, April 2, 1613, the four-year-old son of the noble family of John Ponger, while playing in the courtyard, fell into a pool of water. When his parents reached him, he was dead. The father, a devotee of the Saint, rushed into his living room, where he had hung a painting of the Saint, and falling down on his knees, prayed fervently to the Saint to restore his son to life. When he returned to the courtyard, he found the boy alive and well. In gratitude, the father took his son to the nearby Minimi monastery and had him clothed in the Minimi habit. When he grew to manhood, the boy became a Minimi friar and served the Order long and well.

In 1619, Father Vincenzo Liuzzo in the diocese of Syracuse, Sicily, was dying. His brother recalled that he had been a devoted follower of St. Francis of Paola. He placed an image of the Saint on the priest's breast, and Fr. Liuzzo was immediately restored to health.

The Saint's divine protection also extended to certain cities. On March 27, 1638, on the Saturday before Palm Sunday, an earthquake devastated the Calabrian provinces of Cosenza and Reggio, destroying many homes and other buildings and killing and maiming many people. The quake shook Paola, and the statue of the Saint erected at the entrance of the city was spun around by the tremor until it faced the city. Despite the shock, Paola sustained no noticeable damage, and none of its people was injured. Through the years, Paola survived several other earthquakes that devastated the Calabrian peninsula, including the tremendous earthquakes of 1905 and 1908, which caused great damage to many Calabrian, Neapolitan and

Sicilian cities and killed and injured thousands of people (over 75,000 dead).

In 1598, Sicily was suffering a great drought that had continued for months, withering all crops and vegetation and drying up streams. Toward the end of April, the Bishop of Catania called the people together for a penitential procession to the Church of Saint Francis, where he exhorted them to ask the Calabrian Saint to pray to God to forgive them for their transgressions. A Jesuit, Father Bernardo Colmago, led them in the prayer. Suddenly the skies became clouded and a tremendous rain started falling, lasting for hours, completely restoring the farms and gardens throughout the Island.

In 1625, Naples was being decimated by a cholera epidemic, with scores of people dying every week. On November 11 of that year, the Calabrian Saint was finally established officially as the patron saint of the city in an impressive, solemn ceremony at the Minimi Church of St. Louis. With the end of the special services and prayers to the Saint, the city's epidemic miraculously ended.

On May 27, 1629, an eight-day celebration was held for the new Patron Saint of Naples. It was attended by Cardinal Archbishop Francis Boncompagni, as the Pope's emissary, the Duke of Alba, the Spanish King's viceroy in charge of Naples, secular and religious priests, brothers and nuns, and most of the city's population. At the end of the religious ceremonies and processions, the most magnificent in the city's history, Father Bachelier deposited a cervical bone of the Calabrian Saint in the base of a silver statue of him, which was then transported from the Minimi Church of St. Louis to the city's Cathedral.

The Spanish city of Malaga, which the Saint, through intermediaries, had helped King Ferdinand and Queen Isabella wrest from the Moors, was in the throes of the Black Plague in 1637, with some 15,000 people dying each month. A Spanish Minimi priest, Father Andrea Perez, touched one of the victims with a rosary that had been blessed by St. Francis. He was immediately cured.

Father Perez then touched other victims of the plague with the rosary, achieving the same results. Happy over his discovery, he went to the Archbishop and told him of the miraculous cures. The Archbishop made immediate arrangements for a penitential procession of clergy and people with a statue of St. Francis leading the way. Father Perez walked behind the statue carrying a heavy cross over his shoulders. The people joined in the prayers and the procession to the Minimi Chapel, where a solemn Mass was offered in honor of the Saint. Within three days the plague had left the city. The city named the Calabrian Miracle Worker their patron saint, and each year they honor him on this day of their deliverance.

In France, Lyons was cleared of an epidemic in 1620 through special prayers to St. Francis, and one hundred years later, in 1720, Frejus, the second city the Saint visited in France, was being swept by the Black Plague. On October 20, the city council, at the urging of Minimi priests, voted to celebrate the Saint's feast day with special solemn Masses and penitential processions each year. A few days after this pledge the plague ended.

In the summer of 1706, Turin was being besieged by the French and had been reduced to dire straits. Father Joseph Vico, the vicar-general of the Minimi province, prevailed upon Victor Amadeus, the Duke of Savoy, and the city authorities to declare the Calabrian Saint the patron saint of the city and to participate in a novena to him. The nobility and leaders of the city joined the Duke and the clergy in the novena. During the first eight days, conditions remained the same. On the ninth day, September 7, however, the Turinese army won a sweeping victory over the French, forcing them to lift the siege. The victorious soldiers burst into the churches with cries of triumph as the last part of the novena was being completed, adding their prayers of thanks to those of the priests and people. On October 1, the Duke of Savoy and other leaders of Turin expressed their gratitude for the intervention of the Saint with a triduum [three days] of prayers at the Minimi Church.

King Ferdinand I, Spanish Bourbon ruler of Naples, who was forced out of the city by Napoleon and took refuge in Sicily, made a solemn vow to the Calabrian Saint that if he helped him regain his throne he would erect a great basilica in his honor. Returned to his throne in 1815, he made immediate arrangements to have the basilica built on the very ground on which the Minimi Church of St. Louis had been destroyed by Napoleon's soldiers in 1800. The basilica was completed under his son, Ferdinand II, in 1836. It had been designed by Peter Bianchi, a famous architect of the times from Livorno. Beneath the basilica, he arranged for the tombs for the members of the Neapolitan royal family. Pope Gregory XVI officially designated the building a basilica.

The Saint's determination to be obeyed promptly and fully was made clear in a miracle in 1854 reported in a pastoral letter dated July 8, 1855, from Mgr. Silvia Parladore, Bishop of Ss. Mark and Bisignano.

The Saint appeared to a farmer, Pasquale Servidio of St. Agatha, three nights in succession, May 16, 17 and 18, 1854, asking him to notify the bishop and the priests to offer solemn Masses of reparation and to bless the fields to avoid a pestilence that would devastate the crops. The farmer ignored these appearances and admonitions of the dead Saint as meaningless dreams. The morning after the Saint's fourth appearance, Pasquale went into the fields to carry out his daily chores. Suddenly a Minimi hermit friar appeared from nowhere and walked toward him with a grim face. When he came near, the hermit said sharply: "What has been your obedience? Why did you not relay my message to the clergy? Why hasn't my statue, with that of St. Anthony of Padua, been carried in a solemn procession to the place that I designated? So blindness will make you a believer!" The apparition pulled him with one hand and with the other touched his eyes. Pasquale instantly became blind. Stunned and frightened, he called for help. Neighbors ran to his side, and he told them that a friar had blinded him. The three neighbors that had heeded his cries, Giacinto Piani, Anthony Martorelli and Francis Diodato, saw no one and thought he had had hallucinations. They took him home and advised the parish priest of what had happened. The priest rushed to Pasquale's home. Pasquale told him what had occurred, including the appearance of the Saint of Paola in his dreams for four nights, plus his admonitions. The priest escorted Pasquale to the bishop, to whom he repeated his story.

The bishop called in all the pastors of his diocese so that they too could question Pasquale to determine the accuracy of his story. Two doctors were summoned to establish the fact that the farmer was indeed blind. The next day, Servidio was brought to the cathedral and taken to the altar dedicated to St. Francis. He knelt before the altar in fervent prayer, asking forgiveness of the Saint for his failure to obey him. Instantly his sight was restored. The clergy and people that had crowded into the church beat their breasts and, with tears in their eyes, cried out: "The blind sees again! The blind sees again!"

The next day, after Masses of thanksgiving to the Calabrian Saint, a procession of penance was held, as had been requested by the vision, with his statue and that of St. Anthony of Padua being carried in honor. Priests and people from all the parishes in the diocese participated, and the crops were saved from the threatened destruction.

On March 27, 1943—the birthday of the Saint, who was born in 1416—Pope Pius XII made the Calabrian the "Patron Saint of all Italian Sea Workers." This was because the Saint had been party to many activities involving the sea, including his miraculous passage of the treacherous Strait of Messina on his cloak in 1464.

The Papal decree indicated that the Saint's patronage was to cover all Italian navigation companies, along with all other Italian maritime activities. The seal that designated him as the "Patron of Italian Sea Workers" shows him traversing the Strait of Messina on his cloak with the inscription "St. Francis of Paola, Patron of the People of the Sea." The establishment of the Saint as the Patron of the Sea was celebrated with processions and jubilee Masses in Genoa, despite World War II, then in progress. The Genoese festivities were marked by the ringing of the Bell of the Sea, which was forged in 1930 and blessed by Cardinal Miniretti in the presence of members of the Italian Royal House and leading Genoese political and religious leaders.

In 1948 a pilgrimage was arranged to areas where the Calabrian had worked his miracles. It began at Paola, then went to Catona, Reggio, Messina, Milazzo, and finally Taranto, on the Adriatic. Leaders of the new Italian Republic participated in these ceremonies and in the recitation of the special prayer to St. Francis as Patron of the Sea, approved by the Pope.

The Saint had four nephews and one niece, the children of his sister Brigida. The first of these was Andrea, who came with him to France in 1483 and held important positions in the French court until his death shortly after his uncle was canonized. Andrea married Jacqueline Molandrin, of Blois. They had four children, three of whom joined religious orders, the two boys the Minimi, and the girl the Poor Clares. The fourth child, Francis, was born dumb and with crippled hands and feet. His uncle quickly cured him, and he later became a Minimi and provincial of the Turenne monasteries. The third son, John, held many important court positions, including counselor to the King and head of the Chamber of Counts.

Two of the Saint's nephews, Nicholas and Peter, became Minimi and remained in Calabria, and the girl, Angela, and the youngest nephew, Paul, married and raised families in Paola.

Among the living descendants at the time of this writing is Count Wladimir d'Ormesson, a member of the French Academy and for many years French Ambassador to the Holy See.

The Saint left a number of writings, including three rules, those for the Hermit Friars, the Sisters, and the Third Order of lay men and women, as indicated. These rules were first approved by Alexander VI in 1493, and in their final form under the official Papal seal in 1506 with the title *"Inter Caeteros."* He also wrote the *"Correctorium,"* a code of discipline for the religious, supplementing the Rules, which was approved by Julius II. Also prepared by him are the *"Cerimoniae,"* relating to ceremonial procedures in the Minimi churches and chapels.

Preserved in the Biblioteca Calabra in Naples is a poem by the Saint in eight line stanzas *("ottava rima")* entitled "Passion of the Lord" plus his letters, which were collected and first published in book form in 1615.

To date, St. Francis of Paola has been the subject of more than eighty books—in Latin, Italian, French, Spanish and German—starting with a life written by an anonymous disciple, who is believed to have been a Minimi priest, Father Lorenzo delle Chiave (Clavenses). This was written in Italian and then translated into Latin and French. Till now, there has been no English life of the great Calabrian Miracle Worker (that the authors have found), the principal reason for this book.

The Saint was also the subject of many paintings. The first and most famous of these, now located in the Church of the Most Holy Annunciation in Montaldo Uffugo, near Cosenza, was painted in 1483 by an unknown but skillful Neapolitan artist on orders of King Ferrante. This is considered the most accurate of existing portraits. It shows the Hermit Saint leaning on his staff, dressed in a frayed maroon tunic and hood and wearing simple, one-strap sandals. At that time he was sixty-seven and, as the portrait indicates, in vigourous health. There is a portrait of him in the Prado Gallery at Madrid, the work of the great Spanish painter Murillo. However, the most realistic and impressive is a portrait done in 1632 by G. B. Piazzetta, an Italian. *[Cf. the front cover—Ed.]* In it the Saint looks at the observer with a steady, penetrating gaze. The word *"Caritas"* ("Charity") which summarizes the purpose to which he had dedicated himself, is seen in the upper right hand corner just over his staff.

There are members of the Third Order scattered throughout the United States, Canada and other New World nations. It is to be expected that First Order monasteries and Second Order convents will be established in the American continents some time in the near future.

Today the General House of the Minimi is in Rome and the present Corrector General is Father Francis M. Savarese.

If you have enjoyed this book, consider making your next selection from among the following . . .

Prices guaranteed through December 31, 1993.

At your bookdealer or direct from the publisher.

Prices guaranteed through December 31, 1993.

NOTES

NOTES

NOTES

NOTES